# THE PRACTICAL HANDBOOK OF WALKING & ORIENTEERING

# THE PRACTICAL HANDBOOK OF WALKING & ORIENTEERING

How to cross hills, back country and rough terrain in safety and confidence: a professional manual for hikers, paddlers, horse trekkers and extreme cyclists

PETER G. DRAKE

HERMES HOUSE

**AUTHOR'S DEDICATION**

To my parents, who gave me my first chance to travel to wild places; to Kate who has helped me so much to continue travelling over the last 30 years, and to Neil and Colin who have made some of the expeditions special because they were there with me.

This edition is published by Hermes House, an imprint of Anness Publishing Ltd, Hermes House, 88–89 Blackfriars Road, London SE1 8HA; tel. 020 7401 2077; fax 020 7633 9499

www.hermeshouse.com; www.annesspublishing.com



Publisher: Joanna Lorenz
Editorial Director: Helen Sudell
Senior Editor: Sarah Ainley
Photographer: Martyn Milner
Designer: Nigel Partridge
Illustrator: Peter Bull Art Studio
Editorial Reader: Jay Thundercliffe
Production Manager: Steve Lang

**PUBLISHER'S NOTE**

The author and publisher wish to stress that they strongly advise the use of a helmet and flotation aid in all paddling situations, a close-fitting cycle helmet when cycling, and a secure safety helmet when riding a horse. Travelling in the wilderness is all about taking responsibility for your own decisions, actions and personal safety.

Although the advice and information in this book are believed to be accurate and true at the time of going to press, neither the author nor the publisher can accept any legal responsibility or liability for any errors or omissions that may be made, nor for any inaccuracies nor for any loss, harm or injury that comes about from following instructions or advice in this book.

**ETHICAL TRADING POLICY**

At Anness Publishing we believe that business should be conducted in an ethical and ecologically sustainable way, with respect for the environment and a proper regard to the replacement of the natural resources we employ.

As a publisher, we use a lot of wood pulp in high-quality paper for printing, and that wood commonly comes from spruce trees. We are therefore currently growing more than 750,000 trees in three Scottish forest plantations: Berrymoss (130 hectares/320 acres), West Touxhill (125 hectares/ 305 acres) and Deveron Forest (75 hectares/185 acres). The forests we manage contain more than 3.5 times the number of trees employed each year in making paper for the books we manufacture.

Because of this ongoing ecological investment programme, you, as our customer, can have the pleasure and reassurance of knowing that a tree is being cultivated on your behalf to naturally replace the materials used to make the book you are holding.

Our forestry programme is run in accordance with the UK Woodland Assurance Scheme (UKWAS) and will be certified by the internationally recognized Forest Stewardship Council (FSC). The FSC is a non-government organization dedicated to promoting responsible management of the world's forests. Certification ensures forests are managed in an environmentally sustainable and socially responsible way.

For further information about this scheme, go to www.annesspublishing.com/trees



A CIP catalogue record for this book is available from the British Library.

Previously published as *Walking & Orienteering*

# CONTENTS

# INTRODUCTION

As little as fifty or so years ago, walking and orienteering trips were mostly confined to well-worn beaten paths. 'Off the beaten track' meant just that: the untrodden wilderness areas of the world – places that few people, except the indigenous inhabitants, had any means of exploring. They were virtually the exclusive reserve of a small group of explorers, scientists and travellers, who either needed the backing of large commercial companies or research organizations, or had private means.

Today all this has changed. There are now myriad tour companies which offer adventurous hiking, cycling, canoeing and kayaking trips, and all sorts of treks on horseback and pack animals to take you wherever you would like to go. The huge number of travel programmes on television have made such places seem familiar, while newspaper articles and guidebooks deliver detailed information on almost every country of the world.

▼ *Cross-country skiing offers the adventurous some of the hardest challenges, but also some of the greatest rewards.*

Never has the wide world of adventure travel been so accessible, and this book is designed to help you plan, prepare and participate in the great global outdoors. The first section, *Planning & Preparation*, shows you how to manage a walking or orienteering adventure in remote territory. Included are all the before-you-set-off aspects such as budgets, insurance, the paperwork, medical preparations and personal and mental fitness, as well as the all-important task (these days) of risk assessment.

*Navigation*, the second section, takes you through key orienteering skills such as how to use a map and compass accurately and confidently, and shows you how to orientate yourself in the wilderness using the sun, moon and stars, as well as how to be guided by the weather – crucial in remote areas.

The final section, *Travelling*, explores how you can add cycling, kayaking and canoeing, horse or even camel riding, as well as various off-road vehicle options to your orienteering. This section also includes easy-to-follow advice on the equipment and skills needed for problem-free exploration.

▲ *As part of your orienteering trip you might also plan to travel on horseback to give your weary feet a well-needed rest.*

With this vast freedom to roam, however, come responsibilities. The democratization of travel has meant that the pressure on sometimes fragile environments has increased hundredfold, so that enthusiastic travellers are in danger of destroying the very places they have set out to see. In some cases national authorities have been forced to impose rules and regulations on people wishing to tramp the trails through these magnificent wilderness areas. In some ways this defeats the wish of people to get back to the simpler, more natural life of the wilderness, but it is a balancing act that must be achieved in order to protect the natural world.

As an example of this, we need only consider the base camp area of Mount Everest, where once two or possibly three national expeditions camped each year. Now there are commercial companies taking tens of people up the mountain at a time, and producing large amounts of rubbish and waste in what was once a pristine environment.

In the 1960s you could still visit Mount Kenya or Kilimanjaro, hire your own porter and simply set off up the mountain, so long as you gave your name to the local authority or national park. Now you have to buy into a

▲ *Carrying all your camping equipment on your back allows you to hike along remote and beautiful paths and stop where you like.*

▼ *The leisurely pace of river travel by kayak or canoe offers a unique approach to a region and a close-up view of nature.*

package that provides you with accommodation, guides, porters and food, taking away much of the fun of planning your own expedition. But because of the number who wish to hike up these mountains, there has to be some sort of control or the very wilderness that everybody is seeking would soon disappear.

The era of fast, cheap world travel has, ironically, brought its own set of problems for the adventurous walker and orienteerer. You can leave London or New York and be in the African bush or on the Arctic tundra within 24 hours, but you may not always be prepared either physically or mentally for the environment you find yourself in. This was not the case in the past, when travel was slower and gave one time to adjust to new environments and acclimatize to the cold, heat or altitude. However, there is much that you can do before you travel in terms of training and planning to allow you to make the most of your trip, whether you are travelling on foot, by boat, with animals or in a vehicle.

In this book you will find the skills you need to plan your walking or orienteering trip, and to remain there comfortably and safely and so enjoy these unique environments. There is practical advice on training before you leave, on equipping your expedition and on skills such as navigation, fieldcraft and campcraft. You must also remember that even the best planned expeditions can go wrong, so you should always have a back-up plan. Be realistic about the risks associated with your trip, and always think ahead.

It is hoped that the skills outlined in this book will help to set you on a sure path to adventure, and give you the confidence to walk, hike, bike or canoe your way safely through the wilderness and enjoy these wonderful places.

PETER G. DRAKE

# PLANNING & PREPARATION

Good planning is the key to a successful trip and anticipation is a big part of the pleasure of travelling. Careful preparations mean that everything should run smoothly and problems can be coped with rather than turning into crises. Don't make your plans so rigid that you can't enjoy the unforeseen: be prepared to take a different path or follow up an exciting opportunity that presents itself during your trip.

# Planning your Trip

Some degree of planning is necessary for any kind of trip. The complexity of your planning will depend on factors such as the remoteness of the area, the size of the group, and the length of the trip, but there are several decisions that have to be made in advance for even the most straightforward of outings.

Start the planning by thinking of the type of trip you want to take. When you have decided what this is, you can start to think about the destination, the people who will be going with you, the route, the means of travel, and the length of time you will be away.

You may not be able to make final decisions without doing some research, using maps, guidebooks or the internet, and you may need to adapt or change your plans as you gather information about what is involved. This is why planning is so important. The more thoroughly you think through your ideas and construct your plan, the less chance you have of encountering unexpected problems during your trip.

**DOMESTIC TRIPS**

If you are going on a walking week somewhere in your own country, then choosing your destination and your travelling companions, finding out train times or planning a car journey, calling the local tourist information office for information about campsites and buying suitable maps are the key tasks. You will have to consider what type of clothing and equipment you are likely to need, and if you do not own some of the items already, you may have to borrow or buy them. It is important for safety and comfort that your clothing and equipment are suitable for the climate, and some research into the kind of weather you can expect will prove invaluable.

Depending on the activities you are planning, you may need to buy additional insurance or brush up your skills with some training. Health concerns may need to be addressed, and you should familiarize yourself with basic first aid skills.

▲ *A day's kayaking can give you a new perspective on an area, so check out the range of activities available at your destination.*

◀ *Find out about the terrain and expected weather conditions – how you cope with these is central to the success of your trip.*

**FOREIGN TRIPS**

If you are going further afield, your planning may involve booking trains, ferries or planes, obtaining permits to walk or climb, hiring transport or obtaining paperwork for your vehicle, as well as obtaining visas, vaccinations and an international driving licence – all in addition to the things you need for a domestic trip.

If you are hoping to travel part of your route by cycle, horse or canoe, some practice sessions are a good idea to ensure that potential problems are identified and sorted out before you are out in the field. A cycle touring trip, where the bike is loaded with heavy gear, is very different from a day's cycling in the countryside; and even if you can already ride a horse, if you are planning an expedition on horseback, you need to know how to feed and

**PLANNING AND PREPARATION CHECKLIST**

**12 months ahead**
- Decide on the destination, route and aims of the trip.
- Decide on the group members.
- Think about transport options.
- Think about the activities to be undertaken.
- Carry out your risk assessment.
- Seek permission from countries or places to be visited.
- Produce an outline budget.
- Produce an information sheet on the area to be visited.

**10–12 months ahead**
- Hold the first meeting for the group.
- Finalize the dates of the trips.
- Check that all members have passed any medical examinations required
- Finalize the details of any activities to be undertaken.
- Agree the dates of any training sessions.
- Have a camping weekend with all the people going on your trip.

**8–10 months ahead**
- Finalize the list of equipment needed.
- Draw up a personal equipment list.
- Arrange insurance (medical, personal, third party indemnity, and so on).
- Draw up an outline menu and food requirements.
- Book any ferry crossings, flights, rail tickets, campsites or hotels.
- Appoint a home contact.

**4 months ahead**
- Obtain any visas required.
- Start any vaccination programme required.
- Finalize food and menus.
- Finalize the itinerary for the trip.

**1 month ahead**
- Obtain any additional paperwork.
- Pack all non-perishable food.
- Gather together, check and pack all equipment.
- Check and make ready any vehicles you will be using.
- Send any freight ahead.
- Change money and buy travellers' cheques, if using.

**1 week ahead**
- Complete all vaccination programmes; start to take malaria tablets, if appropriate.
- Check all equipment and food against lists.
- Check all passports and other travel documentation.
- Go through the complete itinerary with the home contact.

**1 day ahead**
- Check your tickets.
- Check your kit and make sure you have packed everything.
- Check with the airport, ferry port or train station that there has been no change or delay to your transport plans.
- Make sure your hand luggage does not have anything in it that will cause you problems at airport security checks.

care for the horses at night. If you are travelling to a remote area and will be a long way from professional medical services, your first aid preparations need to be substantial. You may have to follow a vaccination programme before you travel, and you will need to take considerably more with you in your first-aid kit. In terms of first aid skills, a wider knowledge is invaluable for expeditions to remote areas or involving higher-risk activities, such as mountaineering: in the event of an accident, your chances of survival are far greater if you know what to do.

For such an expedition, planning should start at least 12 months before the trip. The checklist shown above is one that you may find useful. It is only a starting point, and you may find that you can leave some of the items out and/or add some of your own.

► *An off-road cycling trip can be hard going, and a programme of fitness training may be necessary for several months before you travel.*

# First Thoughts

There are many different aspects to consider when organizing a trip in the wilderness, and numerous detailed plans need to be made. The enormity of the project can seem very daunting when you first begin to think it through, but if you break the task down and deal with each aspect one by one, the planning will be easier to manage and you will soon find that you have resolved all the issues.

▼ *Children can greatly enjoy a trip to the wilderness, but make sure you make your plans for the trip with them in mind.*

### THE TEAM

If you are choosing a team, think about the number of people that will work best for the activities you are planning. If it is a large group, it may be a good idea to have a designated leader. Choose your travelling companions with care and bear in mind that people react in different ways to the pressures of life in the wilderness. The group needs to be compatible, with roughly equal levels of fitness. Encourage individuals to talk about what they hope to gain from the experience: taking on board everyone's comments and establishing objectives is the first step in the organizational strategy. If team members do not know each other in advance, plan a trial camping weekend to see how you all get along. For more information, see the section Getting your Team Together.

### BUDGET

Once your plans have been drafted, you need to work out a realistic budget. It is important to do this early on so that you can amend your plans to fit the budget if the total works out to be more than you want to spend. Do not underestimate costs and include a contingency fund of at least 15 per cent of the total. For more information, see the section Planning the Budget.

### INSURANCE

Never overlook insurance, and make sure you are covered for the activities you are planning, as well as for your life, health and possessions in the area you are visiting. For more information, see the section Money and Insurance.

### EQUIPMENT

A list of personal and group equipment can be drawn up only once you have chosen the team and decided where you are travelling to, when you are going, and what you are going to do when you get there. Clothing and equipment must be appropriate for the climate and your planned activities.

### MEDICAL PROVISIONS AND FITNESS

If you are in doubt about whether there will be reasonable access to medical help in the area you are travelling to, you may prefer to have someone in the team with reliable first aid knowledge; discuss the most appropriate type of training with your team. Check if you need vaccinations or any particular medication, such as malaria tablets, and consider what level of fitness the team will require for the activities you have planned. For more information, see the section Medical Preparations.

**PLANNING FOR A GROUP**

You may be planning a trip for an existing group of people – your family, for example – and this might mean that you need to accommodate a fairly wide range of abilities and interests.

- If you are travelling with children, make sure you know their limits and don't push them too hard.
- Keep your plans flexible and be ready to compromise: tired, irritable children will wreck everyone's day. If you are crossing time zones, give children plenty of time to adapt.
- Build some rest days into your itinerary. The strongest, fittest members of the group can use these days for additional, more challenging excursions if they wish, returning to camp to meet up with the group in the evening.

**TRANSPORT**

Consider how best to transport the team and all of its equipment to your destination. Bear in mind that the means of travel will affect the amount of luggage you can take with you.

If your trip is being planned as a simple loop, starting and finishing in the same place, you can drive to the location and leave your car (or hire car) for when you get back, or you may be able to arrange a pick-up from a family member or friend. Depending on the size of the group, you may find it easier (particularly with a group of young people) and more enjoyable to hire a multi-seater vehicle and travel together, rather than make your own way there in individual cars.

If you are planning to travel by public transport, check that there is a connecting service all the way to the start of the route, and work out how you will get there if there isn't. If you require seat reservations – which is advisable for a larger group of people – you will need to book early. Be prepared for departure delays or cancellations, with a contingency plan and a budget in case you are faced with unexpected accommodation costs. Check that you will be able to carry bulky equipment such as bicycles or kayaks and all the related gear. If travelling by plane, find out about the weight allowance and the penalty that you will be liable to pay if you exceed it. If you are taking a vehicle abroad, see the section Vehicle-related Paperwork.

▲ *Some team members may see the trip as a chance for relaxation, while others may be making plans for an action-packed adventure. Find out what individuals expect to gain from the trip so that you can plan accordingly.*

▼ *Travelling by plane will affect the amount of equipment you can carry, so your means of transport should be one of your first decisions.*

# Getting your Team Together

Having the right people in your team will add to the enjoyment of your trip and will help to make it a more valuable experience. Suitable travelling companions are as important as the right equipment, and they need to be given just as much thought.

### CHOOSING AN OBJECTIVE

Whether you are planning a trip with family members, or with friends, or as part of a team of new acquaintances, encourage people to communicate their expectations and goals for the trip before you go, and try to synchronize these goals into a common objective for the team. A shared objective is a good incentive that will encourage cohesion in the group. Spend time discussing likely situations and deal with concerns until you have a clear objective that you can all feel happy with, and one that is well within the capabilities of everyone.

### CHOOSING TEAM MEMBERS

If you have an idea for a trip and are now choosing others to go with you, pick people with whom you get along and who have a level of experience similar to your own. Make sure they are compatible with each other, and seem happy with the idea of teamwork and group decision-making, and that they share your objectives for the trip.

If you need individuals with specific skills, such as first aid, be clear about their level of skill and check that their training is up to date; if it is not, ask them to take a refresher course.

A similar level of physical and mental fitness across the team is important. It may seem unkind to reject someone because of ill-health or injury, but an unfit person can slow down and even endanger the whole group. If conditions will be demanding, consider whether individuals are up to the challenge, or will turn out to be complainers.

**PROMOTING TEAM SPIRIT**

- Encourage team members to write a list of personal goals while you are still at the early planning stages, and try to build their aims into the schedule to encourage their commitment.
- Get an agreement on rules from the whole group before you set off, to avoid misunderstandings and conflict on the expedition.
- A trial camping weekend is a good way to see how a new group gets on together. It will encourage team bonding, and will also identify any problem personalities while there is time to do something about them.

▼ *A shared agenda, common goals and compatible personalities among the team are key features for a successful trip.*

► *Good communication is essential, and leaders need to talk to the group at least once a day to keep everybody informed.*

## LEADERSHIP

For a trip involving a large group of people, it is a good idea to have a leader. This person can be self-appointed or chosen by the group, but he or she must command sufficient respect to be able to direct the group under good and bad conditions. The leader role is especially important with a group of children, or when travelling in unfamiliar or difficult terrain, or if the planned activities require a specific skill or experience.

With a group of adult friends, the leadership role can be informal, but for a group of above 20 people, a bigger leadership structure may be needed, and other team members can be asked to take responsibility for particular concerns, such as driving or first aid.

### Communication

This is the most important skill a leader can exercise. A leader needs sound judgement and has to be able to lead discussions and communicate effectively, delegate tasks, and act as a mediator in the event of disagreement or conflict. Communication is especially important when people are in difficult conditions and possibly suffering stress and panic. If communication fails, members will at best become dissatisfied and the whole trip may become an unhappy experience. At worst, the group may come to grief.

### Personality problems

A clash of personalities needs to be sorted out as soon as possible (preferably before you leave if you spot it that soon). If the group starts to break up into cliques, its common objective will become more difficult to achieve. Fun bonding activities, such as team games, can help to restore team spirit.

Always avoid showing favouritism. If it is noticed, some individuals may feel undervalued, and it could act as a spark for bad behaviour or aggression.

#### POSSIBLE ROLES FOR TEAM MEMBERS

The list below gives an idea of the different areas of responsibility that exist within a team. You may need only some of these in your group.

**Deputy leader**
To take over from the leader if anything happens to him or her before or during the trip.

**Quartermaster**
To be responsible for all equipment and food, and for looking after and issuing these throughout the trip.

**Field treasurer**
To approve the final budget, record all expenditure in the field and make sure the money lasts for the duration of the trip; may also be in charge of safeguarding funds and valuables.

**Head of camp kitchen**
To appoint a daily team and organize a rota to carry out food preparation, cooking, and washing-up duties, to oversee those duties and to draw up appropriate daily menus.

**Medic or first aider**
To treat team injuries and illnesses during the trip, and to look after the group first-aid kit; for larger groups, to keep a record of allergies or intolerances and any prescription medication being taken by anyone in the team; to record any illness or accidents that happen during the trip and the treatment given; could also be responsible for pre-expedition medical check-ups, vaccination programmes and fitness sessions.

**Navigator**
To look after and carry the maps and compass, to advise on the planning of the route, and to ensure that all team members follow the correct route.

**Translator**
To communicate on behalf of the group when travelling in a foreign country with a native language different to your own. Someone who can understand a handful of phrases and key words is enormously useful.

# Planning the Budget

The first task when you are planning the finances for a trip is to work out how much money you will need. The next task is to decide how the money is going to be spent. For both of these processes you will need a budget. The budget outline here is a starting point to which you can add or subtract headings to suit your trip.

▲ *Even a simple backpacking trip involves costs, and you need to think about every aspect of the trip to plan a useful budget.*

### BEING REALISTIC

Make your budget realistic and err on the side of caution, so that you can be confident you will be able to pay for all aspects of the trip. If you are worrying about money while you are away, your enjoyment will suffer.

Plan your budget in advance to give you time to research the costs fully. If you cannot get confirmed prices, get as many estimates as you can. Note the best price (lowest) and the worst price (highest) and budget in between the two. Ideally, the budgeted figures will work out just about right or too high. If they don't, you will have to dip into your contingency fund to cover basic expenditure, such as food, transport and accommodation, and there will be less money available for an emergency that necessitates a sudden change of plan.

### BUDGET OUTLINE

**Administration**
- Postage
- Telephone/fax/internet charges
- Publicity
- Passports and visas

**Equipment**
- Buy
- Hire

**Training**
- Canoeing or kayaking/horse riding/cycling/skiing
- First aid

**Transport**
- Plane/ferry/train/bus/taxi
- Vehicle hire
- Animal hire

**Freight**
- Equipment
- Vehicles

**Insurance**
- Personal
- Vehicle

**Bank charges**
- Currency changing
- Bank transfers

**Food**
- Buy at home
- Buy abroad

**Field expenses**
- Living costs
- Hire of guides/local people
- Fuel
- Customs and port duty
- Gifts
- Miscellaneous

**Post-expedition expenses**
- Administration
- Photography

**15% contingency fund**

### BANK FEES

If you need to buy foreign currency, plan for bank charges for money changing and for transferring money abroad. If you have opened a bank account for the trip, budget for the charges that apply to any account.

### FOOD AND EQUIPMENT

If travelling by public transport, check that you will not exceed the baggage allowance on your ticket, as this can incur charges. Goods can be freighted, but this can be expensive, and getting through customs can be costly in terms of money and time. Find out if it would be cheaper to buy food and equipment at your destination.

### CONTINGENCY

Like insurance, this is essential. Allow at least 15 per cent if your trip will include vehicle transport, as you may need to pay cash for mechanical repairs.

# Money and Insurance

When planning any kind of expedition, you need to consider the safest and most convenient way of carrying money. Make sure you have adequate insurance cover for all of your planned activities.

## MONEY

There are a number of ways to take the money you will need in the field. Try to pay for as much as possible in advance, so that you do not have the additional risk of carrying large sums of money with you.

### Travellers' cheques

These are far less tempting to thieves because they can be used only with a passport as proof of identification. Buy travellers' cheques in the currency of your destination or, if these are not available, in the currency most acceptable there. A mixture of small and large denominations is the most useful. People and businesses in rural areas and in some developing countries do not accept travellers' cheques as payment, and it will be necessary to take cash in the local currency with you as well.

### Cash restrictions

In some countries, in order to control the income generated by tourism, it is necessary to change a certain amount of money per person into the local currency, and you may not be allowed to change it back again or to take it out of the country. Find out if such rules apply at your destination before you travel, and budget accordingly.

### Credit cards

You may not be able to use credit cards outside larger centres of population or international hotels, and check service charges and exchange rates before using credit cards to withdraw cash from ATMs abroad. Company credit cards are available for services such as car hire. International car hire companies issue them, and anything spent on the card is billed to you in your own currency, which makes it easier to check what has been spent.

## INSURANCE

Standard holiday insurance will cover your needs for most trips, but you may need to take out specialist insurance for more adventurous activities.

### Personal accident insurance

Standard holiday insurance will usually include a pay-out for personal accident claims, but ensure that it gives adequate cover for death, loss of a limb or sight.

### Medical insurance

If you are going to an area with inadequate or non-existent medical services, air ambulance cover will be essential. You may also require separate rescue insurance if you plan to be in a remote or mountainous area, or if you are sea-touring in a canoe or kayak.

### Baggage insurance

Most holiday insurance policies include an amount for delayed or lost baggage. Expensive items such as cameras and jewellery should be properly insured; avoid taking valuable items that are not necessary for the trip. Household insurance may cover some items, but always read the small print on your policy before you travel.

### Credit card insurance

Always be insured against the loss or theft of credit cards because cards are such an obvious target for thieves.

▼ *Even if you intend to carry travellers' cheques and credit cards, you should still take some cash in small denominations.*

Note the telephone number of the lost or stolen card department of your card issuer and keep it with you in a safe place, separate from your credit card.

### Hazardous pursuits insurance

Winter sports, mountaineering, boating, diving, big game hunting and other hazardous pursuits usually require specific insurance, even if you are not travelling abroad. Check the details of your standard holiday insurance policy to see what it will and will not include. As there is a greater risk of injury with these activities, insurance is essential.

### Third-party insurance

It is sensible to have this in case, for any reason, you harm, or even kill, someone, or cause damage to their property. Third-party insurance is usually included in standard holiday policies, but check before you travel.

### Vehicle insurance

If you are hiring a vehicle or taking your own with you, make sure you have sufficient cover for the country you will be driving in, as well as any countries you may need to drive through to get there.

### Light aircraft insurance

If your plans include flying in a light aircraft, check that you are covered with your personal accident insurance. If you will be flying the aircraft yourself, it may count as a hazardous pursuit and require separate insurance.

# Risk Assessment

As a member of a team, you have a responsibility to yourself and to the other members of your team. It is essential to assess the possible risks that any activity undertaken on the trip could bring, where team members might be harmed and how high the level of risk is.

▲ *An off-road mountain biking trip seems like a low-risk activity, but the potential for injury is high, especially for novices.*

**WHY ASSESS RISK?**

Risk assessment is the evaluation of an activity to determine what could go wrong, who could be hurt and what could be done to manage the identified problems. Accidents will happen, but efficient risk assessment will reduce the potential for accidents and enable lessons to be learned from near misses and actual incidents.

**IDENTIFYING HAZARDS**

Mentally step back from the activity and look at it from a fresh point of view, concentrating on those aspects that could result in serious harm. Ask people who are unfamiliar with the activity what they think, as they might identify areas not immediately obvious to a regular practitioner. Equipment manufacturers' instructions may also help you to identify hazards and risks.

You should take into account other potential hazards, too, including natural disasters, extreme weather conditions, acclimatization to high altitude, dangerous wildlife and the safety of local drinking water. If mountain rescue services could be needed, check that they will be available. Be aware of medical/health hazards and make sure that everyone has had the necessary inoculations. A good guidebook should be able to provide this information. Your journey may take you into a politically unstable area, where civil war, guerrilla warfare, kidnapping for ransom, or terrorist activity may be a threat. Foreign office websites will usually have the most up-to-date and reliable information.

▼ *A good guidebook can highlight potential dangers in a region, but check foreign office websites for the latest and most reliable information.*

When undertaking any activity, those most obviously at risk are the participants and their instructors, but you also need to gauge the potential for harm to those waiting to take part, spectators and passers-by.

**EVALUATING RISK**

Having identified the separate elements of the activity, you need to assign a level of risk to each element. Grade the level of risk from high to moderate or low, and take into account the past history of the activity, which may include actual incidents as well as any near misses.

A change of operating technique, additional equipment or increased training might be all that is needed to reduce the level of risk and therefore improve safety, without eliminating the

▼ *Guerrilla warfare presents a serious risk to personal safety: it is advisable to change your plans if this appears to be a hazard.*

element of challenge. Check the small print of your insurance policies (personal, vehicle and group policies) to be sure you have a level of cover that reflects the risk involved.

▲ *Basic training before the trip is advisable for activities such as canoeing, where some knowledge of the skills will improve safety.*

▼ *Fitness and discipline are important in mountain country or on rough terrain, where careless accidents can easily happen.*

**RECORD KEEPING**

Keep records of when equipment and facilities to be used by your team were acquired (new or used), their service history, any repairs or changes, and incidents that happen on your trip. The records should be made available to any other people who may wish to use the equipment in the future.

**ASSESSMENT PROCEDURE**

- Look at the hazards.
- Decide who may be harmed and how.
- Evaluate the risks arising from the hazards and decide whether existing procedures are adequate or if more should be done.
- Record your findings.
- Consult your risk assessment during your trip, and revise as necessary.
- Review your assessment after your trip and revise as necessary.

# Personal Paperwork

Paperwork may not be the most exciting part of travel, but it is vitally important. If you arrive at a border or get stopped by the police, you could be in real trouble if you do not have the correct personal documents.

### PASSPORT

Make sure you have at least six months of life left on your passport if you are going to a country where you require a visa. Most visas will require at least a half page and in many cases a full page of your passport, so make sure you have sufficient pages empty in your passport.

Some countries issue passports with more than the normal number of pages in them, so if you are completing lots of international travel, especially to countries that require visas, it is worth considering getting one of these. Otherwise, if the normal one runs out of pages before it has expired, you will have to pay for another passport.

### VISAS

These are a way for a country to control who gets into it and, in some cases, to make money from visitors and tourists. Visa regulations are constantly under review as immigration policies change and are revised from time to time.

You should telephone the embassy of the country you wish to visit while you are still in your own country, or contact its website on the internet, to find out if you will need a visa.

Visas for which you need to make an application can be obtained from the relevant embassy in your own country, either in person or by post. Depending on your nationality, your reason for travel and your destination, the issuing time can vary from hours to weeks. If you are sending your passport and visa application, plus the fee, by post, make sure you use a registered postal service and make a note of your passport number or photocopy the information pages of your passport before you post it. To get into some countries, you will also need to be sponsored by someone already living and working there. Always make sure you read the requirements of a visa very carefully because if you get it wrong and are refused entry, you may never be allowed a visa again.

If you are already abroad, you will usually be able to get your visa from the appropriate embassy in a neighbouring country. This can take time: in some cases, up to several weeks. Do not lose your patience with the embassy system or its staff; it will not speed up the process and it could lead to further delays, if not a refusal of the visa.

This is one instance where it pays to plan ahead. Decide if you are going to visit any country for which you need a visa while you are planning your trip. This will allow you plenty of time to apply for the visa(s) while you are still at home.

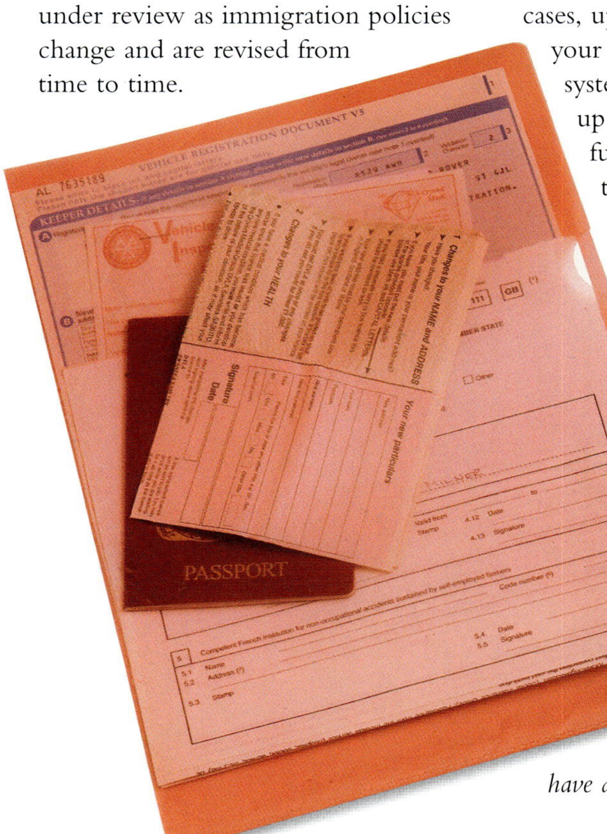


◄ *Keep your passport and other papers secure, not only while travelling but also between trips, as they have a high value on the black market.*

**PAPERWORK CHECKLIST**

- Passport
- Visas
- Driving licence
- International driving permit
- Record of vaccinations
- International certificate of vaccination
- International camping carnet
- Currency and valuables documents

### DRIVING LICENCE

Take a photocopy of your national driving licence, even if you know that you need an international driving permit to drive abroad. A national licence with your photograph on it will be accepted by most car hire companies abroad as a form of identification and proof of your ability to drive.

### INTERNATIONAL DRIVING PERMIT

This document is recognized worldwide as proof that you hold a valid driving licence in your own country. The international driving permit (IDP) does not have to be carried as a legal requirement for foreign drivers in every country, because many countries recognize each others' licences, but it is intended to help motorists driving abroad, where licence requirements can vary widely, and it can be an advantage to be able to produce it if you run into difficulties with the transport authorities. It may also be a useful form of pictured identification in the case of a lost or stolen passport.

The international driving permit is printed in 10 languages – the five official languages of the United Nations (English, French, Spanish, Russian and Chinese) plus German, Arabic, Italian, Swedish and Portuguese. It is available, on payment of a small fee, from motoring organizations in the country in which your national driving licence was issued.

**RECORD OF VACCINATIONS**

Medical organizations and even some airlines now issue booklets in which you can record all the vaccinations you have had and when you had them. These are a convenient reminder to keep vaccinations up to date and they may also provide some sort of proof, if they are in a semi-official booklet, to a border guard or local doctor that you have received the vaccinations. If you do not have a booklet, note the vaccinations you have had and when you had them on a piece of paper and keep it with your passport.

**INTERNATIONAL CERTIFICATE OF VACCINATION**

Also known as the Yellow Card, this is internationally recognized proof that you have immunization against certain diseases, including measles, mumps, rubella, typhoid, hepatitis A, yellow fever and polio – all of which are recommended if you are travelling to developing countries or to rural or undeveloped areas of developed countries. It is issued by the doctor or medical organization that gave you the vaccination. Make sure the certificate is properly filled in and date-stamped with the official stamp of the centre, otherwise it may not be accepted. In some countries, you may be asked for the certificate at the border; if you do not have it, you will usually be offered the vaccination on the spot – to be administered by non-medical staff working in poor conditions and with a risk of dirty needles – or no entry.

**INTERNATIONAL CAMPING CARNET**

This document is issued by camping organizations worldwide, and has your passport details added to it. At many campsites you may be able to hand it in instead of your passport, which allows you to keep your passport for changing money, cashing travellers' cheques or any other reason, including peace of mind. Campsites are not obliged to accept the carnet in place of your passport, so find out in advance what the policy is at the campsites you intend to use.

**CURRENCY DECLARATION**

In some countries, a declaration of foreign currency has to be filled in at the border. This covers high-value items such as cameras and jewellery as well as money. Though it won't always happen, the documents can be requested when you leave the country, to check you haven't sold the items, so fill them in correctly and do not lose them.

▲ *Visa requirements vary widely between countries, depending on your nationality. Check foreign office websites for the latest information regarding what you need.*

▼ *If you are planning to paddle on rivers or lakes, check that the water has unlimited public access and you are not trespassing on private land, particularly when you are abroad or unfamiliar with local by-laws.*

# Vehicle-related Paperwork

If you are planning to take a vehicle abroad with you, you should allow time to assemble all the relevant paperwork that is needed in addition to your national and international driving licences. In some countries, you could run into serious difficulties if you are stopped by the police without the correct documentation, and a lack of adequate insurance could be disastrous in the event of a breakdown or accident.

Vehicle-related documents are usually issued by driving organizations in your own country. If you are unsure about what you will need contact one of these organizations for up-to-date advice before you travel.

**REGISTRATION DOCUMENTS**

These documents will be required to prove ownership of the vehicle you are driving if you are stopped by the police or if you try to cross a national border.

**INSURANCE PAPERS**

Always carry the original paperwork for the insurance cover you have in your own country, and make sure the policy is valid. If you are taking your vehicle abroad, international insurance is available from national motoring organizations and insurance companies.

Additional protection is provided by the Green Card, which is recognized in over 40 countries (mostly in Europe, but including Russia, Iraq and Iran) as part of a United Nations system to protect motorists abroad. The Green Card does not provide insurance cover but is proof that the requirements for third-party liability insurance in the countries for which the Green Card is valid are covered by the motorist's insurance policy in their own country. Contact motoring organizations in your own country to find out if you are eligible and for further details.

**PAPERWORK CHECKLIST**

- Driving licence
- International driving licence
- Registration documents
- Motor insurance
- International certificate for motor vehicles
- Letter of authority
- Customs carnet

**INTERNATIONAL CERTIFICATE FOR MOTOR VEHICLES**

This is a vehicle passport and is valid for one year. It gives the registration document information in a number of different languages. Although the number of countries that accept it is limited, it is worth having for its translation of the information about the vehicle – which you may find useful if you need to visit a garage for mechanical repairs and you don't speak the local language. It also provides a way of recording your vehicle entering and leaving a country.

**LETTER OF AUTHORITY**

If you are driving a vehicle of which you are not the owner, such as a hire car, you will require a letter from the owner or the hire company stating your registration details, that you have their permission to drive the vehicle, and in what countries you will be travelling.

**CUSTOMS CARNET**

In some countries, you will be required to have a customs carnet to take a vehicle from one country to another, and to avoid having to pay customs duty on the vehicle. When you arrive at the border on leaving or entering, your papers will be checked and you will be asked to put up a bond – ostensibly to cover the cost of the customs duty, although the bond can be up to several times the cost of the

◀ *There are many advantages to travelling in your own vehicle, but you could run into difficulties without the correct paperwork.*

vehicle – before the carnet will be issued. Contact the relevant embassy before you travel to find out if a customs carnet is needed and how much the bond will be.

▲ *Vehicle-related documents can be kept in the car, but store them in a safe place away from other gear, and keep copies separately.*

▼ *It can be useful to carry an itemized list of valuable equipment, such as work or study equipment, to produce at border crossings.*

**COPIES OF PAPERWORK**

Take photocopies of all vehicle-related paperwork and keep them separate from the originals, so that if the latter are lost or stolen, you will still have proof of your entitlement to drive the vehicle. It may also be useful to carry a few passport photographs in the vehicle, as well as photocopies of the information pages of your passport.

If you are carrying valuable, bulky or unusual equipment in your vehicle, it can be a good idea to have a list of the items to produce when crossing borders. If you can get the list stamped in advance by the embassy of the country you are entering, it can help to smooth your way through customs.

# Medical Preparations

Part of your preparation before the trip is to find out which medical issues might affect the team and how you should protect yourselves. The medical problems you are most likely to encounter will vary depending on your destination. Follow the advice given in up-to-date guidebooks to the region you are visiting and contact specialist medical organizations for current advice and guidelines.

Your family doctor will be best placed to answer any questions relating to your current physical health and how it may be affected by, for example, changes of diet or extreme climatic conditions. A vaccination programme can guard against some of the endemic disease hazards, while specialist clothing or sleeping nets will help to protect you from the insects that carry the diseases. In other cases, you will be able to avoid ill-health or injury by knowing of potential risks and adapting your behaviour accordingly. You also need to know what medical facilities and emergency services will be available in the area you are visiting, and if you will be entitled to use them free of charge.

**HEALTH WARNING**

Some health conditions can cause serious complications while you are away. You are advised to seek medical advice about the suitability of your trip if any of the following conditions apply to you:

- Existing serious injuries
- Asthma
- Epilepsy
- Migraine
- Pregnancy
- High blood pressure
- Heart disease
- Cancer
- Contagious diseases

## VACCINATIONS

Before you leave, everybody going on the trip should have all the vaccinations specifically required for the area you are travelling to, which could include meningitis, rabies, hepatitis A and B, yellow fever and tuberculosis, as well as the standard polio, tetanus (sometimes given with diptheria) and typhoid vaccinations that you may already have.

Individual team members must be responsible for checking whether they need boosters of previous vaccinations, but you may need to provide the relevant information and remind them to make sure they are adequately protected. If you are travelling with children or young people, liaise with their parents or guardians to get vaccinations organized. Everyone should make sure that all the necessary vaccination certificates are in order.

Depending on your destination, malaria tablets may be necessary, and you will need to find out well in advance about when to start the course of tablets. Your family doctor or travel agent may not have this information or be fully up to date, and it may be preferable to contact a medical organization that specializes in endemic and tropical diseases, and has the latest information available for travellers. Many airline companies also offer a vaccination advisory service.

◀ *A good level of health and physical fitness will make a walking trip more enjoyable, and can help to safeguard you against injury.*

### CHECK-UPS

Have a full medical check-up before you travel if you are going away for a long time, or if you are travelling to a developing country or to an undeveloped region of a developed country where the medical services may not be as good as they are at home, or if you know that medical care will be very expensive.

If a qualified doctor or medic is to accompany you on the trip, they could be asked to carry out check-ups on team members. Individuals should also be asked to fill in a questionnaire regarding their past medical history, any prescribed medication they currently take, and any drugs or foods to which they are allergic.

The parents or guardians of children or young people should be asked for this information on their children's behalf, and should sign a form giving permission for medication to be given to the child in an emergency.

Ensure that all team members have a reasonable standard of physical fitness. This will help them to acclimatize to the more difficult living conditions outdoors, and will make them less prone to injury. Anyone in doubt about an ongoing health issue should talk to their own doctor before they travel. If you feel that an individual's condition could pose a risk to the rest of the team you may need to ask them to drop out.

### DENTAL CARE

Persistent toothache will spoil your trip and if you are going to be away for more than a couple of weeks neglected tooth decay could lead to an abscess, infection and even blood poisoning. Have a dental check-up before you travel if you have not visited the dentist recently, and leave enough time for any treatment that proves necessary to be completed before you travel. If you are going to a high altitude or to a very cold country, local climatic conditions can bring on severe toothache in any unfilled cavities.

**HEALTH WARNING**

Your personal safety is at risk if you do not take adequate measures for existing medical conditions or against contracting disease.

▲ *If you are heading for a remote area where you know that medical services will not be available, you must make sure you take with you all that you need for any existing medical conditions, as well as an adequate stock of first aid supplies and medication for everyday ailments.*

► *Learn as much as you can about the conditions you will be living in, and think about how this will impact on your health.*

# Medical and First-aid Kits

The size and type of your first-aid or medical kits will depend on the nature of your expedition, the amount of time you will be away and the standard of your first aid or medical training.

If you will be doing a range of activities during the course of your trip, or will be travelling in different climates, you may need a greater range of first aid items or even a number of different kits to be fully prepared. Larger groups will have the capacity to carry a more comprehensive medical kit, kept in a vehicle or at the base camp, which caters for everything up to minor operations. Even so, basic first-aid kits still need to be carried by individuals, so that they can give first aid care in the field.

### WHAT TO INCLUDE

When deciding on the size of the kit and what to put in it, think about the conditions in the area, the potential for risk of the activities being planned and the kind of accidents that may happen.

If you feel you need informed advice about what to include for an informal trip or with a small group, buy a standard first-aid kit and take it to your family doctor or to a specialist organization; ask them for suggestions of additional items and non-prescription drugs to include. One such item may be an emollient cream such as zinc and castor oil, which is useful for common skin conditions such as sweat rashes.

### STANDARD FIRST AID ITEMS

- Plasters and adhesive dressings
- Sterile dressings
- Gauze pads
- Crêpe bandages
- Thermometer
- Small pair of scissors
- Sterile scalpel
- Safety pins
- Disposable gloves

Larger groups may have a designated first aider or medically trained person, whose responsibility it will be to compile an appropriate medical kit. A standard kit will then be all that individual team members need to carry as part of their own personal equipment.

If you are travelling to a part of the world where AIDS is a major threat, or where you are not sure of the standard of medical care, include a sterile needle kit in case injections are needed. Keep the contents sealed in the case provided, so that they remain sterile and if your luggage is opened by customs officials or police you cannot be accused of using the needles for drugs.

Whatever the size of your medical or first-aid kit, make sure that all items are kept clean and are clearly labelled and easy to identify. If you need to use the kit in an emergency situation, you will want to find what you are looking for quickly.

▲ *Having assembled your first-aid kit, make sure that the contents are labelled and well organized, and that the kit is always kept clean and dry.*

### KEY FIRST AID SKILLS

Before your trip, attend a first aid course or a refresher course to learn or brush up on procedures for the following medical conditions. (For further information see the section Emergency First Aid.)

- Resuscitation
- Recovery position
- Choking
- Shock
- Drowning
- Bites and stings
- Wounds
- Animal, reptile and insect bites
- Burns and scalds
- Sprains
- Fractures
- Effects of hot weather and cold weather

**FIRST AID PRINCIPLES**

**Know your kit**
It is immediately reassuring for an injury victim if you can produce a well-equipped first-aid kit when you give them treatment. It will also help you to handle the situation with confidence if you know that you have certain essential items with you. However, it is vital that you are familiar with the items in your kit. This includes knowing what they are, what to use them for, and how to use them correctly.

**Practical knowledge**
The casualty will feel calmer if you can dress and bandage an injury quickly and professionally, but if you become flustered and need to keep unwrapping the bandage to start again, they will start to panic.

**Think on your feet**
Nothing in your first-aid kit is as important as your ability to act swiftly and improvise with whatever materials you have to hand, while constantly reassuring the casualty to prevent panic.

**Making contact**
Communication with the outside world can be a key factor in dealing with a serious first aid situation. Focus on making the best use of whatever is available – passers-by, telephones or air and sea rescue services. Learn the international signalling codes, and be confident that you can give an accurate grid reference to locate your exact position. One day, somebody's life may depend on it.

▲ *Activities such as cycling introduce injury risks that can be prepared for if they have been identified in your risk assessment.*

▼ *Accidents can happen in any situation, and you need to be aware of the potential hazards in the environment you will be in.*

## FIRST AID TRAINING

At least one person in the team should have a good standard of up-to-date basic first aid training, but all team members can be encouraged to familiarize themselves with key first aid skills. There is no doubt that the more people in the team with first aid training, the safer the trip will be for all.

If the risk assessment has highlighted any particular areas of risk associated with your destination or activity, consider what specific training the first aider may need, such as how to treat snake bite, hypothermia, frostbite, heat stroke, dehydration or drowning. For health issues relating to specific activities, it's sensible to contact a specialist organization for advice and possible additional training.

Find out as much as possible about the medical facilities available at your destination. This kind of information is available from guidebooks, tourist information services and possibly from the relevant embassy. You will need to know the standard of local hospitals, where the nearest major towns and cities are, and the quickest way to get to them from a rural area; whether there is a 24-hour accident and emergency facility and how good it is, and how you would go about getting an airlift rescue if someone became seriously ill or injured. The more basic and inaccessible the medical facilities, the more comprehensive your medical kit and training need to be.

# Physical Fitness

The level of personal fitness you should have for your trip will depend on what the trip entails. If you are planning some mountain biking or white-water canoeing, for example, you will need a more advanced level of fitness than if you are planning low-level walking, though you should still be physically fit and mentally prepared.

If you are travelling as part of a team, remember that you have a responsibility to the other team members to stay as fit and healthy as you can. One person's ill health or lack of fitness may cause problems and could endanger the rest of the group. Regular, gentle exercise every day for at least a month before the trip will help to protect you against illness and injury.

### ALL-ROUND FITNESS AND PERFORMANCE

To achieve a level of all-round physical fitness appropriate for camping trips and outdoor activities, the following components are essential: endurance; strength; flexibility; speed; agility; balance; coordination; and reaction time. Of these, endurance and flexibility are the most relevant here.

▲ *Swimming provides an excellent workout, building stamina and promoting all-round fitness without straining any of the muscles.*

### ENDURANCE

This means being able to continue physical activity for a long time, and it is the most important component of fitness. The fitter the person, the greater the level of endurance. There are two different types of endurance: cardiovascular and muscular.

#### Cardiovascular endurance

This involves the lungs, the heart, the blood and the blood vessels. It is the ability to exercise the whole body for long periods of time without running out of breath or becoming tired.

To build up your cardiovascular performance, work out a plan to undertake a series of fairly vigorous physical exercises that will make the heart work harder. Swimming is an excellent form of fitness training because it exercises muscles throughout the body. Particularly good are the backstroke and the butterfly, as these give a good workout to the back and shoulder muscles, which can be difficult to exercise by other means. Cycling and running are also very good for improving all-round fitness and stamina, and they are especially good for the big thigh muscles. As part of your exercise plan in the build-up period up to a month before your trip, do some regular training in the boots or other clothing you will be wearing on the expedition, in order to get used to them. Wearing a backpack that is packed with the same weight as you will carry on your trip is very useful.

◀ *Cycling is good cardiovascular endurance training, and is very effective for the large powerful muscles in the thighs.*

▶ *Running will help to build up your stamina, but wear suitable footwear to protect yourself against impact injuries.*

**WARNING SIGNS**

Consult your doctor before beginning an exercise programme. Stop exercising if you experience any of the following:

- Chest pain
- Dizziness or confusion
- Nausea or vomiting
- Cramping pains in the legs
- Continued breathlessness
- Continued fatigue
- Palpitations
- Fluid retention

### Muscular endurance

This is the ability to use the same muscles repeatedly without getting tired. Different activities require skills in different areas and therefore the development of different muscles and joints. For example, a walking and climbing trip needs strength in the upper and lower parts of the legs. If you need to carry your own camping and cooking equipment in a pack on your back, the shoulder muscles will also need to be strong. A canoeing trip, by contrast, needs strength in the arms, shoulders and chest, while a cycling trip needs strong upper and lower legs and strong arms and shoulders.

▲ *Diagonal crunches, from the elbow to the knee, will help to tone the stomach muscles and increase upper-body strength.*

You can tone your muscles and improve body strength in many ways. You may find it convenient to join a fitness club, where there is professional equipment, and follow a simple but regular programme of targeted action, supplemented with regular walking carrying a backpack. Alternatively, press-ups, pull-ups and stomach crunches are good exercises to prepare you for outdoor activities, and these can be done at home without the need for fitness clubs or sports equipment.

▲ *(Top) The simple press-up is an exercise to build short, powerful muscles in the pectoral, biceps and triceps areas of the body.*

▲ *(Above) You may find that by supporting your weight with your knees, you will find it easier to do press-up repetitions.*

▼ *Pull-ups are a good way to promote arm strength. Build up the number of repetitions as your muscles get stronger.*

### TESTING YOUR FITNESS

Regular exercise will improve your fitness and endurance and make you feel better and livelier in every way. You will soon notice the difference in your general health, but some simple tests can help you measure your progress and provide extra motivation to keep going.

- As aerobic exercise strengthens your heart it will pump more slowly and efficiently. To take a step test, step on and off an exercise bench or step about 30cm (12in) high. Step up with one foot, placing it fully on the step, follow with the other, then step down with one foot followed by the other. Maintain a steady pace for three minutes, then check your pulse immediately. An average rate for a man might be between 100–110 beats per minute and between 110–120 for a woman. Compare your results over time to see how your heart rate drops as your fitness improves.
- Measure upper body strength by doing press-ups. Simply do as many repetitions as you can to the point of exhaustion. Keep a record of your total and aim to beat it.
- Measure abdominal strength by doing stomach crunches: see how many you can do in one minute.
- Measure lower body strength with squats: do as many as you can, working at a steady pace, and see how your score builds up as you work out regularly.

▶ *A gentle jog along a beach is just one way to warm up your muscles before you begin a programme of stretching exercises.*

**FLEXIBILITY**

Stretching and mobilizing joints and muscles is a vital way to increase your range of movement and to prevent muscle strain. Always start a stretching programme with 15 minutes of gentle warm-ups, such as a brisk walk with your arms swinging, a game of frisbee, or a jog, to prepare your body for sudden exertions and minimize the risk of muscle injury.

Practise simple stretches on their own to achieve a good all-round level of flexibility, or practise them after endurance training to increase the benefit of a workout. Start at the top of the body, with stretches for the head and neck, and work down towards the legs and feet. Never bounce to increase your range of movement, but extend yourself gently to the limit of comfort. Hold each stretch for at least 15 seconds before relaxing. The longer you stretch your muscles after a workout, the more flexibility you will attain.

▼ *Stand with your feet apart, and one hand on your hip. Raise your other arm above your head and lean slowly across to gently stretch your side. Repeat on the opposite side.*

▼ *Stand with your feet together, then bend one leg back from the knee and grasp the foot to stretch the hamstring and quadriceps. Repeat with your other leg.*

▼ *Stand with your feet together, then bend forwards, keeping your back straight, and raise your arms above your back. Join your hands together and hold for 15 seconds.*

▶ *Having confidence in your ability to cope with difficult challenges makes you more likely to achieve your goals.*

**MENTAL FITNESS**

Strength of mind comes from within and is founded on your belief in yourself to cope with any situation you find yourself in. Knowing that you have prepared well helps you to overcome mental anxiety, and feeling that you are strong and fit, and that your physical strength can see you through times of difficulty, means that you are less likely to feel anxious about living outdoors.

Preparing in advance for emergency situations is invaluable. Training will make you more able to cope with hardship and difficult conditions, both physically and mentally, and it will improve your awareness of your abilities and limitations, which will increase your confidence. In the rare event that something does go seriously wrong, it will make you less likely to panic.

**MENTAL PREPARATION**

Some people who are well prepared physically for a trip do not perform well when they get into the field. This is largely due to a lack of mental preparation, which leaves them unable to adjust to their new surroundings or unprepared for what they are going to see or come into contact with.

Some people find the lack of privacy in camp a problem; others are upset by the poverty or sickness they may see around them in a developing country, or the smells and sounds they will encounter. Some people find it threatening to sleep out in the open and prefer to be in a tent: if one isn't available, they may not sleep well.

Many such problems can be eased by finding out as much as possible in advance about the area and culture you are going to, and trying out new experiences before setting off, such as cooking over a wood fire for the first time, or doing a difficult climb. These things can seem strange and threatening when you first do them, but will seem less so the next time. It is usually fear of the unknown that makes us most uncomfortable, not the experience itself.

**FOOD AND TEAM MORALE**

Food plays a key role in team morale when you are living outdoors, where the evening meal is a welcome treat at the end of a long, tiring day in the field. A healthy appetite is a sign of a positive attitude, and if the team is eating, it is also receiving the energy supplies it needs for strenuous activity.

However, eating with gusto is not easy after several days on a diet of dehydrated food. This kind of food can cause constipation, which means discomfort, and the lack of flavour can make it very unappealing. If the team doesn't eat properly, energy levels get depleted and individuals can become lethargic and irritable; this makes team spirit sink further still, and problems can flare up as individuals become discontented.

Make sure the team knows what food rations to expect, so that they can prepare themselves mentally for any hardship. Let them try out the rations at a trial camping weekend, and consider how you can improve the food if you feel it may have a negative effect on the team's morale.

# Travelling as a Group

A group expedition involves a great deal of organization to ensure that everyone has a safe and enjoyable trip. The purpose of the trip and an itinerary need to be agreed by everyone before you travel. This is important even for recreational holidays if the trip is to live up to individual expectations and you are to avoid disputes.

### ORGANIZING GROUP MEMBERS

The larger the group, the greater the potential for chaos and confusion, and, not surprisingly, this is especially true with a group of children or young people. Travelling in large numbers can cause problems at ticket offices and check-in desks during the journey, where other passengers can become annoyed by the delays caused by a large group in front of them. Group leaders should remind everyone to get money, passports and tickets ready in plenty of time when approaching a border.

If your group is large, having a list of everyone's names, addresses, dates of birth and passport numbers will help when booking into accommodation or passing through borders. A list of just their names will also be useful for checking that everybody is present when you change modes of transport.

If the group is travelling by public transport, brief everyone on where they are heading and arrange a meeting point at the destination, so that if anyone does become separated, they will still be able to find the rest of the group.

You will quickly learn as the trip progresses which people take much more time to get ready than others, or never seem to have the necessary documents to hand. If they are not to hold up the others, they must be encouraged to be prompt and prepared. Other members of the group can be asked to help make sure they are at the right place at the right time.

### GROUP IMPACT

If you are travelling in a group, and especially if you are acting as leader, it is important to remember that you have a responsibility not only to keep the group harmonious and happy, but to make sure that everyone respects the places and people you are visiting. Groups, especially large ones, can have a substantial impact on fragile environments, and a lack of understanding of the region's culture may cause distress and anger among local people, so good discipline is essential in camp. Before setting off, relay all the information you can about your destination to the team, and make sure everyone agrees to the standards of behaviour they will follow, to make the most of the experience for the whole group.

### DISPUTES

No matter how big or small the party, and how well you know each other, disagreements and personality clashes during the trip are almost inevitable. Having a clear objective for the trip and an itinerary that has been mutually agreed by the group will help to keep these to a minimum, but deal with them quickly when they occur, before the group starts to break into factions.

### CONTINGENCY PLAN

Have a fall-back plan that includes suitable accommodation should you need it at connection points on your journey, in case travel delays mean you miss a connection and are forced to make an unscheduled overnight stop. While individual travellers or a small group can usually be accommodated at short notice, a large group can run into problems if, for example, the flight arrives late, and the vehicle-hire

◀ *For the journey to run smoothly, allocate responsibilities among team members, such as looking out for particular items of kit.*

company has closed for the day. Keep phone numbers for the places you are booked into to hand, in case you need to inform them of any changes. Even if things are going to plan, it is a good idea to give your accommodation a call to make sure all is well for your arrival.

**KEEPING VALUABLES SAFE**

If you are staying in one place for any length of time, try to find a trustworthy individual or organization who will allow you to use their safe. The valuables of an entire group – including passports, travel tickets, expensive items such as jewellery and larger sums of money – can add up to a treasure chest for an opportunistic thief, and for peace of mind it is better to know they are stored safely under lock and key.

**LOST LUGGAGE**

Luggage can and does go missing when travelling, especially on public transport, and this is particularly likely with group travel because individuals tend to be less attentive of shared group equipment than they are of their own belongings. It can help to make one or two people responsible for counting bags at each connection point, to make sure everything travels with you to your destination. If luggage is lost or delayed by an airline, you may have the complication of trying to arrange for it to be sent on to your destination.

▲ *With a large amount of gear and a big camping area, the potential for chaos at a group camp is huge. Encourage individuals to store their own kit tidily when not in use.*

▼ *Essential items of group kit, such as maps or cooking equipment, should be made the responsibility of one or two individuals.*

# Travelling with Young People

For a family camping holiday with your own children, you need to think about how the children will cope with the physical demands of living outdoors and how living in the wilderness may affect their spirit. Be ready to adapt your plans if the children appear uncomfortable or unhappy with the daily routine. Otherwise, as a parent, your responsibilities will be no different to those on any other family trip.

When you take a group of children or teenagers on an organized trip, you and any other leaders are responsible for them the whole time they are away from home. Much of the advice on travelling in a group will apply here, but your position of authority and your ability to deal with young people will make this a different type of challenge.

## GROUP EXPEDITIONS

There should be at least one adult to every six young people, and if your programme includes activities that are potentially hazardous, or if the group members are under 15 years old, then the ratio will have to be higher. If there are children in the group with special needs, the number of adults has to be assessed on a case-by-case basis.

### LEADING YOUNG PEOPLE

The challenges of outdoor living and adventure can be particularly beneficial for children and young people, but youth leaders need to be sure that they minimize the risks inherent in such activities and fulfil any legal requirements arising from their responsibilities. Guidelines are published by national and local education authorities, as well as international youth organizations such as Young Explorers Trust and the Scout Association.

## PRE-TRIP MEETINGS

The agenda for the trip needs to be established with a series of meetings before you set off. The children's parents will want to feel informed and confident that their children are in safe hands. These meetings also allow the leaders to identify problematic issues while there is still time to amend plans.

### Introductory meeting

Arrange a meeting early in the planning stage at which you can give the group and their parents or guardians detailed information about the area you will be visiting and even some training in the activities you hope to carry out there. This may also be the first time the group members meet each other. Explain the rules of behaviour for the trip and detail what will happen to any member who behaves badly.

Collect next-of-kin contact details from each person, as well as three passport photographs. If the group is travelling abroad you will need photocopies of passports and birth certificates in case any passports get lost. You will also need to talk through your insurance policy for the trip.

Ask the parents or guardians of any members under the official adult age to sign a consent form stating that you can authorize medical treatment in the event of an emergency. You also need medical information from every person, including details of any medication and any allergies to drugs or foodstuffs, as well as details of foods that they cannot eat on medical or religious grounds. If the group is travelling abroad, you will need to check that everyone has had the appropriate vaccinations.

### Final meeting

Have a final meeting before you leave to run through the final risk assessment and explain what you are doing about the risks highlighted, pass on any last-minute information and answer any questions. Finally, introduce the liaison agent, who will be the point of contact between the group and the parents or guardians while you are away.

## DURING THE JOURNEY

For a group of up to 12 children, have a rota so that one leader is in charge for a set time while the others relax. Larger groups of children (say, more than 20) are easier to handle if they are divided up into small units, each with its own leader, during the journey.

◄ *An early morning meeting to talk about the plans for the day ahead will make everybody in the team feel involved.*

If travelling by boat or train, or while waiting at an airport, and if the children are old enough to be trusted to behave sensibly on their own, they can be allowed time without adult supervision. Find a fixed point, such as a café, where a leader will be and where passports, tickets and luggage can be left, and ask each child to report in every hour. Keep a list of names to hand so that you can check everyone off as you change modes of transport.

**DURING THE EXPEDITION**

Start each day with a half-hour briefing session on the day's events, and give children the chance to ask questions or express concerns about any aspect of the trip. How much the children can achieve in one day will vary according to their age, physical strength and the type of activities planned. Base your schedule on past expeditions with young people of the same age, and be prepared to revise it if the group does not respond well to the challenges or if unforeseen weather conditions make the original plan untenable.

Deal with instances of bad behaviour immediately. Repeated bad behaviour may result in a child being sent home, but this is a last resort since a leader will have to accompany them, involving extra costs and the temporary lack of a leader.

▲ *Activities such as skiing should be within the capabilities of the child to avoid them becoming anxious or uncooperative.*

▼ *Allow time for rest and play to make sure young children do not overexert themselves.*

# Travelling Alone

Many people love the freedom of travelling alone and relish facing new challenges and seeing new places with just themselves for company. If you hate the thought of group travel, with all the organization involved, the inevitable personality clashes and the lack of spontaneity, then it is worth considering this option.

The greatest advantage of travelling alone is that you have the flexibility of being able to change your plans as and when you want to, without having to consult anybody else. However, there are disadvantages to solo travel, and it is worth bearing in mind the following points when deciding whether or not to take a camping trip on your own.

### BEING SELF-SUFFICIENT

If you are backpacking, you will have to carry everything yourself, including all of your camping and cooking equipment, so select lightweight gear and avoid taking unnecessary items. If you don't already own your equipment, try to borrow or hire as many of the expensive items as you can, or else kitting yourself out will be very costly. Make sure you know how to use all of your equipment correctly – including putting up your tent on your own – and learn how to carry out emergency repairs and maintenance.

### TRAVEL COSTS

Unless you are travelling in your own vehicle and sleeping at a campsite, you may have to pay more for your trip, as ferries and organized trips will often charge a single-person supplement, especially if you want your own cabin or hotel room. If travelling on your own by train in parts of the developing world, bear in mind that a first-class ticket is worth considering from the point of view of safety and comfort.

### KEEPING IN TOUCH

Make a point of phoning someone at home on a regular basis, perhaps at the same time each week, to let them know you are well and what your plans are for the days ahead (emailing is less reliable as the service is not available everywhere). If travelling in a developing country on your own, consider making your country's political representative in the country aware that you are there.

### ACCOMMODATION

The thought of waking up on your own in the middle of the wilderness may seem appealing, but think very carefully about whether you want to be this isolated. Unless you are an experienced camper, a designated camping area may be a better option. Not only is there more chance of finding drinking water and washroom facilities, there will also be like-minded people nearby should you need help or advice, and it will usually be safer. If you are planning to stay in a hostel or hotel on your own, check guidebooks or ask at a tourist information office to find out about the character of the area. When travelling alone it is usually safer to choose accommodation in a better part of town.

**TIPS FOR LONE TRAVELLERS**

Travelling alone can sometimes be daunting but there are sensible ways to minimize the risks:

- Don't dress like a tourist, with a camera slung round your neck.
- Dress conservatively and avoid expensive clothes and jewellery.
- When you meet new people be selective about whom you tell you are alone. If in doubt, pretend you are with friends or a group.
- Don't tell strangers where you are staying: if you are arranging a meeting with a new friend, make it in a public place.
- If you drink alcohol, don't drink too much and don't leave your drink unattended.
- If you are out in a city after dark, stay on well-lit streets.

▼ *Lone travellers have the flexibility to please themselves and change their plans at will if new opportunities arise.*

▲ *Women travelling alone are easy targets for sexual harassment. Be aware of this and make reducing the risk your top priority.*

◄ *Travelling without backup from other people makes you more vulnerable, so plan carefully to minimize the risks.*

**SOLO ACTIVITIES**

If you are planning a walking, cycling, horse riding or driving trip on your own, tell someone what you are doing, the route you are taking and when you expect to return. If you have an accident, they may be your only hope of help. Think very carefully about the wisdom of snow walking, climbing or mountaineering on your own, especially if there is a chance of bad weather. Some activities, such as kayaking and canoeing, should never be done solo. If you want to visit a famous site, consider joining an organized tour or getting a group of like-minded people to go together. It will be cheaper and it could be safer than going alone.

**DRUG SMUGGLING**

As a lone traveller, be careful whom you make friends with and never accept parcels or gifts unless you know what is in them, especially if you are passing through a national border. There are a number of people in prison around the world who carried a parcel for a "friend" that turned out to contain drugs or other contraband.

**WOMEN TRAVELLERS**

Observing local codes of behaviour is a matter of courtesy for all travellers, but for women it is easy to send out the wrong message, especially when travelling alone in countries where an unaccompanied female may be an unusual sight. Outside Europe, Australia and the United States, skimpy or tight clothes, including trousers, are generally inappropriate. Check the conventions before you go and always dress conservatively in loose-fitting, presentable clothes.

All lone women may face some sexual harassment. Take the same precautions you would at home: don't wander up dark alleys alone or accept drinks from strangers; find another woman to sit next to on a bus or train. If you are groped, don't get involved in an angry confrontation but get the attention of onlookers, who will probably rush to your defence. Avoid eye contact with men in public places: wearing dark glasses can help. Time your arrival in a new place during the day, so you are not wandering about late at night: travelling by night can be a good idea if it means you reach your destination in the morning.

On the plus side, local people – women particularly – will be more likely to offer you hospitality. They might assume that a male traveller can cope alone, while you need a helping hand, and they won't see a lone woman as a threat.

Be prepared for your periods to be irregular – changes in time zones, stress and exhaustion can affect them – and remember that stomach upsets can interfere with oral contraception. Sanitary protection may be hard to buy locally, and tampons with applicators are more hygienic in the absence of clean water to wash your hands. Be aware of cultural attitudes – in some countries menstruating woman are forbidden to enter religious buildings or to touch, or even go near, food, so be discreet.

# NAVIGATION

**Knowing how to find your way in unfamilar territory is the most important skill for wilderness travel and it is no exaggeration to say that your life may depend on it. Learn how to use a map and compass before the trip, and train yourself to think in navigational terms, developing an awareness of nature and the landscape around you. This will help you to follow your course and to correct yourself when you go wrong.**

# Maps

◀ *Choose maps carefully, making sure they are for the right area and to a scale that will give you all the information you need.*

A map is a flat pictorial representation of a complex, multi-dimensional landscape. Maps range from rough artistic representations that look nice on the wall, through to very accurate, perfectly drawn masterpieces. The accuracy of maps varies dramatically from country to country, and unless you have previous knowledge of the map you are using you must always treat them as potentially suspect. You will need to use very different maps if you are planning an overland journey from one country to another than if you are planning a walking expedition in a mountain range. Good quality maps are usually dated and list revisions; always check the date when the map was last surveyed or updated, and if a map is old be prepared to make allowances in your navigation.

**SCALE**

The choice of scale depends entirely on what you want the map to show. If you are planning an expedition across a number of countries, then a map with a scale of 1:2,500,000 (25km to 1cm/40 miles to 1in) might be sufficient. If, however, you want a map for a walking expedition then considerably more detail is required.

**MAP SCALES AND THEIR USES**

| Scale | Use |
|---|---|
| 1:15,000 | Orienteering |
| 1:25,000 | Walking (detailed) |
| 1:50,000 | Walking or climbing |
| 1:100,000 | Cycling, trekking, canoeing or kayaking |
| 1:250,000 | Motoring |
| 1:1,000,000 | Map of country |

For serious cross-country navigation in difficult terrain, maps of 1:50,000 or 1:25,000 scale are desirable. The 1:50,000 scale is the most practical for longer journeys as it covers a relatively large area and lacks the intense clutter often found on 1:25,000 scale maps. The 1:25,000 scale comes into its own in very difficult conditions – for example, darkness, white-out or very dangerous mountain terrain.

Often the scale and accuracy of the available maps of an area you are operating in are not ideal and in these circumstances you may have to modify your approach to navigation.

**SYMBOLS**

Every map will show both natural and man-made features. Waterways, roads, railways and areas of habitation will tend to dominate on larger scale maps because these are designed to show a more detailed picture of the area; do not expect to find this amount of detail on smaller scale maps.

Both natural and man-made features will be represented by a number of symbols and are usually described by a key on the map. Maps from different countries have very different symbols. Most symbols have some pictorial link to the feature they represent but always check the key, if it exists, as some symbols can be quite obscure. If something is marked on a map it is likely to exist on the ground, but many things that exist on the ground are not necessarily marked on the map.

▼ *A map with a scale of 1:25,000 means that every 1km is represented by 4cm of map space, which allows a lot of detail.*

▼ *A 1:50,000 scale means that 1km is equal to 2cm, and this makes it easy to measure distances of hundreds of metres.*

▼ *Very large scale maps, such as a town plan, may be useful if you need to navigate your way through an urban area.*

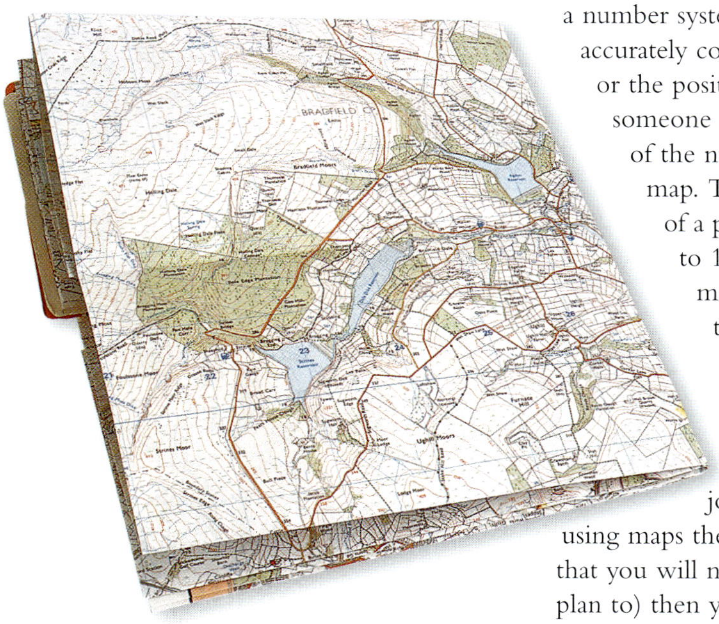

▲ *The information provided on a map enables you to build up a three-dimensional visual picture of the landscape it covers.*

### RELIEF

On some maps different colours show different land heights, and on others the steep sides of hills are shaded to bring the map alive. On large scale maps contour lines are lines of equal altitude and create a picture of the terrain. Typically, contour lines on large scale maps are at 10–20m/30–60ft intervals. This interval does vary so make sure you check before making any important calculations. The ability to look at contour lines on a map and to visualize what the ground will look like is the key to accurate map-to-ground interpretation. Obviously the closer the contour lines, the steeper the country. You can quickly work out how steep the ground is by measuring the distance then counting the contour lines over that distance. You can then work out the ratio of the two in your head or draw a rough scale drawing.

### GRID SYSTEMS

On many large scale maps you will find a series of numbered or lettered grid lines running north to south and east to west. Grid systems are nationally based and, usually, they bear no relation to the system of an adjacent country.

Most grid systems are based on 1-kilometre squares and allow you to name a particular square through a number system. This allows you to accurately communicate your position or the position of a feature to someone else, using a coordinate of the numbers printed on the map. To increase the accuracy of a position from 1 kilometre to 100 metres or 10 metres more numbers are added to the coordinate.

If you think you may need to use grid references during the course of your journey (and if you are using maps there is always the chance that you will need to, even if you don't plan to) then you must familiarize yourself with the system in operation in that area prior to setting off. In the absence of a grid system latitude and longitude are used, again with the position being given as a coordinate of the references.

### TYPES OF MAP

The following are examples of the most common types and scales of map used for travelling. Topographical maps are usually produced by government agencies. They were originally military in origin and are the most accurate maps available. They are checked and updated on a regular basis; if you are buying a map from a map or book store, it is worth checking that it is as recent a revision as possible.

Privately produced maps must be treated with caution unless you have actually used them in the area and are experienced in how to read them. They are often produced primarily for information only, and are not as accurate or as reliable as a standard topographical map. Privately produced maps may not be drawn to scale and may be of a pictorial nature. If this is the case they are unsuitable for serious navigation and should be regarded as for interest only.

In some parts of the world, such as developing countries or in remote parts of developed countries, poor quality maps will be the only ones available and you will have to adopt a far more exploratory approach to navigation.

#### National maps (1:1,000,000)

These are useful for calculating the size of an undertaking or for getting an understanding of where various places are in relation to each other. They show the general outline of countries, their borders, major cities and towns, and major roads and rivers. With this very sparse level of detail, bear in mind that, depending on the country featured, a line on the map denoting a road could mean anything from a six-lane highway to a rutted dirt track.

#### Regional maps (1:250,000)

These are essentially road maps and are not suitable for serious off-road navigation. They can be useful for initial inspiration and planning. They will tend to feature smaller centres of population and minor roads. Sometimes they will show major areas of mountainous country and large areas of forest or jungle.

#### Specialized maps (1:50,000)

If available then these are the best maps for travel in wilderness terrain. They give all the information required to plan and navigate a safe route. At this scale they will normally be topographical maps based on accurate contour lines. They will show detailed geographical features, such as cliffs and rock outcrops, along with accurately mapped vegetation. They will also feature footpaths and forest tracks.

#### Large scale maps (1:15,000)

These are almost too accurate for the purpose of navigation and wilderness travel. They are large and difficult to handle, and they cover a very small land area in a tremendous amount of detail. It is difficult to visualize the country portrayed on the map as the contour lines have broad intervals, and this has the effect of "flattening" the land. Large scale maps can be overly cluttered with information, which makes them difficult to read and interpret for the walker or traveller. However, they are very useful in difficult conditions, such as poor visibility, when intricate detail can be extremely helpful.

# Reading a Map

For thousands of years man navigated successfully all over the world over land and sea without the aid of maps. The luxury of accurate maps that we have become used to is a relatively recent development and really only goes back a couple of hundred years. The reassurance of accurate maps has made navigation as much more accurate art, but the ability to read maps well, interpret them and then apply the information gleaned from them, is still a skill that must be learned and developed for your own safety.

▲ *Geographical features in the landscape can be checked off against the map to make sure you are where you should be.*

**THE THREE NORTHS**

Most national and regional maps are drawn with true north (the direction of the geographic North Pole) at the top. Large scale maps with a grid system, however, use grid north. The difference between grid north and true north occurs because a map is a flat illustration of the Earth's curved surface. In low to mid latitudes the difference between true and grid north can be disregarded, but at high latitudes it becomes significant. The third north is magnetic north. A compass needle does not point to the geographic North Pole but to the magnetic North Pole, which is currently in Hudson Bay, northern Canada, and moves slowly but continually. All quality maps will have all three norths – true, grid and magnetic north – marked on them, along with the annual rate of change of the magnetic variation.

**MAGNETIC VARIATION**

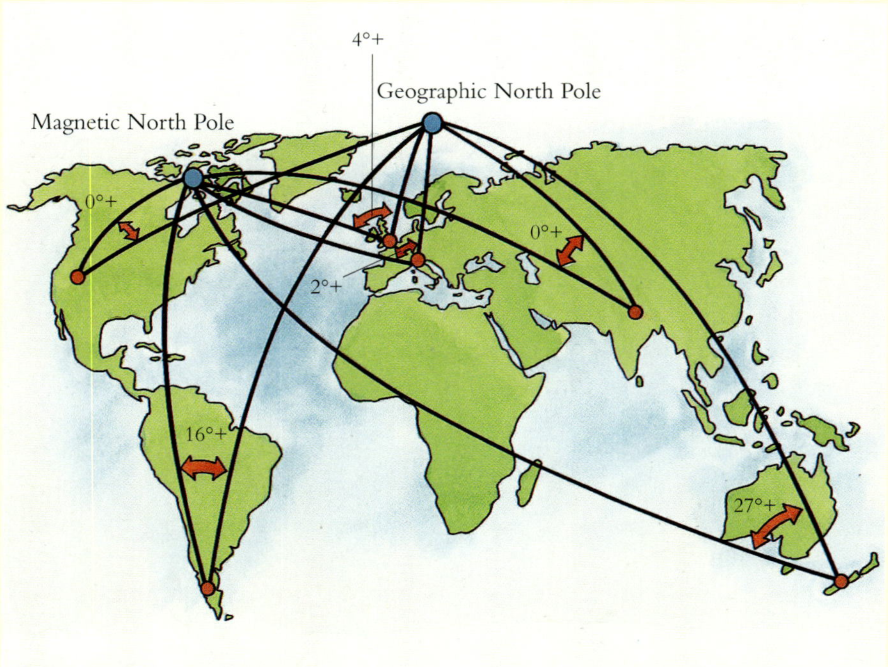


**LEARNING MAP SYMBOLS**

A list of symbols used on the map is usually printed on it in a key. Symbols do vary from map to map so be careful to check before making decisions regarding route choice and distance. You should make yourself familiar with the symbols on the map you are using so that you do not have to continually refer back to the key. This makes map reading fluid and allows you to really see the land as you look at the map. An understanding of and ability to interpret contours is the most important skill of map reading. It is not an easy skill and needs practice to get it right.

If you are not familiar with map reading, spend time practising before your journey until you can read the map with reasonable accuracy. Look at a map of your local area – preferably an area with height variation in the form of hills, and including some natural and man-made features. Choose a route to follow on foot, looking at the contours to assess height variation and noting the features you would expect to find. Then take your map outdoors and follow the route to see how accurate you were.

**A PICTURE OF THE LANDSCAPE**

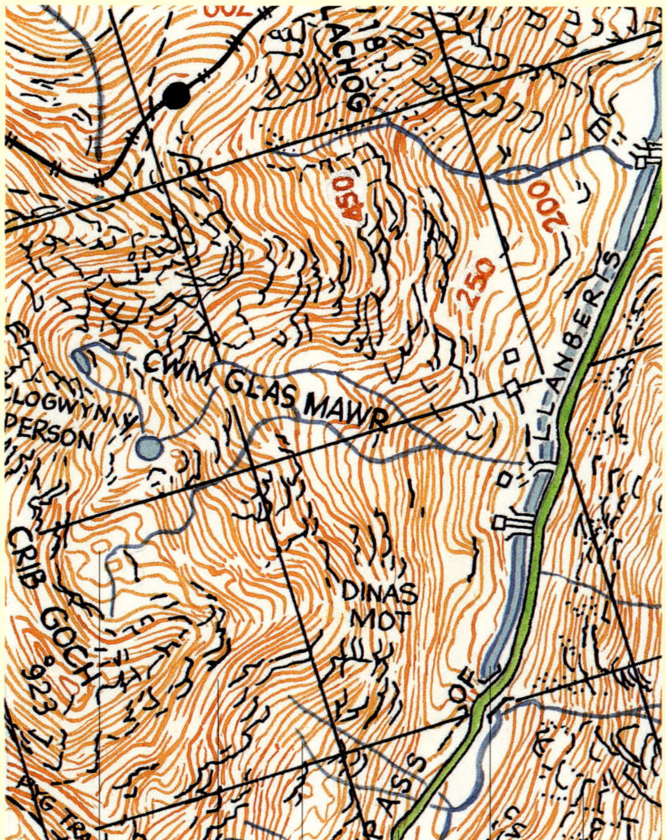

Fully formed contour lines indicate the highest point of the mountain

Contour lines close together indicate a steep area of mountainside

Tributary stream

Road

River

Rocky outcrop

The map and photograph do not bear much relation to each other at a quick glance. You must pick out and identify features in relationship to each other in order to relate the view to the map. Learning to make allowance for areas of land that are hidden from view and to get a grasp of scale are both very important. This is a simple exercise but it will help you to understand the basic principles of reading a map.

Start slowly, identifying features in the landscape and using their symbols to locate them on the map. Focus on one feature at a time, and note how the steepness of the hills is shown by the densely packed contour lines. As you progress, you will begin to see how closely the landscape in the photograph has been represented in pictorial form on the map.

**FINDING YOUR LOCATION**

Good navigators can always relocate quickly and accurately. It is always done by a systematic process of positively identifying and positively eliminating features in the surrounding landscape. The first thing to do is to orientate your map. This can be done visually by lining up the map with features that you can see around you, such as a forest or a lake, or by using your compass (see the section The Compass). Either way, your map will now be pointing north and mimicking the landscape. You can then set about finding features that fit with where you are and eliminating the places you could not possibly be. For example: you are standing on a steep, rocky slope that faces south, looking down on a stream with an S-bend and the stream is flowing east. This immediately eliminates all the slopes that don't face south and all streams that don't flow east. This may leave you with a few possibilities, but continue your process of elimination: how many of the other east-flowing streams have S-bends below a steep rocky south-facing slope? If you are unlucky and there are two you need only find one other distinct feature and you are sure to reduce your possible location to a single choice.

# The Compass

The development and use of compasses to help maintain direction of travel goes back thousands of years. Contrary to what a lot of people imagine, a compass needle does not point to the geographic North Pole but aligns itself along the magnetic field of the earth, pointing to the magnetic North Pole, which is currently situated in Hudson Bay in northern Canada.

Compasses were traditionally a swing needle housed in a round case with the 360 degrees of the circle and the cardinal points (north, south, east and west) marked in order to give a bearing. Later, sighting prisms were added to increase the accuracy of the bearing. In order to take a bearing off a map a protractor had to be carried to measure the angle of travel in relation to the North Pole. After the Second World War the Scandinavians came up with the combined instrument that is almost universally thought of today as a compass. This is a combination of a compass, protractor and a ruler.

The protractor compass is perhaps the most popular type of modern compass. It is a versatile navigation tool which allows you do the following:

- Orientate a map.
- Measure distances on the map.
- Work out a grid reference for the location where you are or for a specified location on your route.
- Take a bearing directly from the ground in front of you.
- Take a bearing from a map, apply magnetic variation (see the section Reading a Map), and follow the bearing to your destination.

### LOOKING AFTER YOUR COMPASS

A compass is a delicate instrument that could save your life. Keep your compass safe, and do not drop it or stand on it. Keeping it strapped to your wrist or worn around your neck on a cord is a sensible option. Do not allow your compass to come into contact with a magnet as this could damage it and will drastically affect its accuracy.

▼ *The modern compass includes a sighting mirror, which allows you to set a bearing by sighting on a distant object in the landscape.*

### AN IMPROVISED COMPASS

A sewing needle that is repeatedly stroked in *only* one direction against a piece of silk will become magnetized and can be suspended on a piece of string or thread so that it swings to north. Top up often to maintain the magnetism. Stroking the needle with a magnet, if you have one, would be even more effective than silk. Stroke the metal in one direction *only*.

### FINDING NORTH

Hold the compass flat in your hand and make sure there is no large source of ferrous metal nearby (this may act like a magnet and attract the compass needle, thereby affecting the accuracy of the reading). The red magnetic compass needle will point towards magnetic north. In order to find true (geographic) north, you will need to know the magnetic variation for the area where you are and apply this to the protractor. Depending on where you are on the earth you may have to add or subtract the variation: your map will be able to tell you which. Line up the red magnetic needle with the lines on the base plate of the protractor; the direction of travel arrow will now be pointing at true north.

### FOLLOWING A BEARING

If there is an absence of line features along your route, such as a footpath, stream or ridge that you can follow to maintain your sense of direction, a compass bearing can act as a reliable substitute, providing a continuous guide to your direction.

Having established the bearing you wish to travel on, line up the red magnetic needle with the lines on the base plate of the protractor; the direction of travel arrow will now be pointing on your bearing. The bearing then has to be laid on to the ground: in other words, you have to identify a feature on the ground, such as a tree,

◄ *The button compass features a magnetic swing needle that shows your location in relation to magnetic north.*

that is in line with the bearing when the compass is held flat in your hand, and walk towards it. Having arrived at the feature, you will need to repeat the process in order to move further along the route. Line up the red magnetic needle with the arrow on the base plate to find your direction of travel, and choose a feature on the ground in that direction. Continue in this way until you reach your destination or are able to pick up a line feature along your route.

In poor visibility it is extremely easy to lose your way and you must avoid drifting off your bearing at all costs. You may have to use ground features that are very close to you to be absolutely safe, such as outcrops of rock or even tufts of grass. If you have other people in your group, you can send one party member ahead to the limit of visibility on your bearing, then ask them to stop and wait until the rest of the party has caught up before sending them off again. If visibility is so poor that you can barely see in front of you, it is an advantage to use a party member as a ground feature because if you call out to them, your voice acts as an indicator of direction and distance; by calling back to you they will be able to direct you to their position relatively easily.

◄ *The prismatic compass is so-named because it contains a prism, which allows for greater accuracy when taking a bearing.*

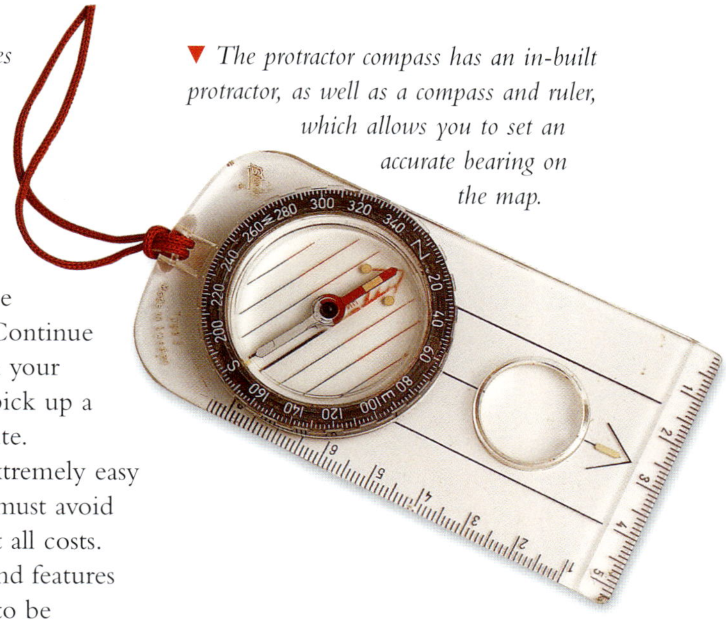

▼ *The protractor compass has an in-built protractor, as well as a compass and ruler, which allows you to set an accurate bearing on the map.*

**HOW TO CARRY A COMPASS**

- All types of compass are sensitive to knocks and shocks, and all must be treated with care when you are on the move. Aim to keep the compass in some form of casing at all times. For easy access, keep the cased compass in the buttoned-up breast pocket of a shirt or jacket, or strapped to your wrist, or worn on a sturdy cord around your neck.
- If travelling by plane as part of the trip, carry your compass in your hand luggage to protect it from the pressure differences of high altitude, which may affect its accuracy. It also means you will not be without your compass if your luggage is lost or delayed.

## LAYING A BEARING TO GROUND

**1** Hold the compass with the direction of travel arrow pointing on your bearing. Select an object in the distance that is in line with your bearing. Walk towards it.

**2** When you arrive at the object, repeat the process to continue along the route. Line up the red magnetic needle with the arrow on the base plate.

**3** With the direction of travel arrow pointing on your bearing, select an object that aligns with the bearing and walk towards it. Repeat as necessary.

# Using a Map and Compass

The essence of navigation is to be able to establish your position anywhere on the earth's surface and then be able to plot a course to another position. Armed with a map and compass a good navigator can confidently navigate in any conditions.

To navigate accurately you need to know your starting point; your direction of travel; and the distance you have travelled. People who get lost have almost always failed to keep track of these three key points, and having done so they then panic and wander around blindly. Re-establishing your position is a matter of quiet, logical observation and slowly proving to yourself that the features you can see in the surrounding landscape fit the position on your map.

**SETTING A MAP TO NORTH**

The ability to orientate a map so that it points north and therefore mimics the land is an easy but important skill. If you can recognize features then you can orientate the map visually. If this is not possible you can use your compass to orientate the map. First you must apply the local magnetic variation to

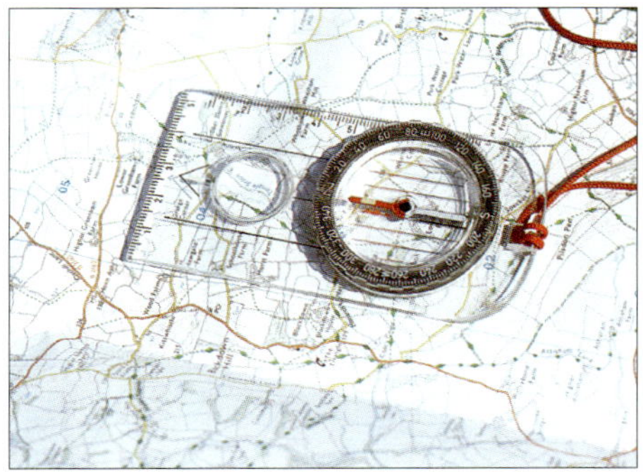

▲ *You need to orientate your map to the land before you set out on the route. Use your compass for this if visibility is poor.*

the compass, then place the compass on the map with the lines on the protractor running parallel to the grid lines on the map. Now move the map around until the red half of the compass needle is in line with the lines on the protractor and pointing north. Your map is now orientated.

**MAP-TO-GROUND INTERPRETATION**

Many navigators rely too much on the use of the compass. This produces a blinkered approach to navigating. The ability to navigate using the map alone gives you a much broader understanding of the landscape you are travelling through and also allows you

**GLOBAL POSITIONING SYSTEM**

The global positioning system (GPS) is an important development in navigational equipment. It can be used for all outdoor pursuits, and is particularly popular for those that cover large distances in remote areas, such as kayaking, cycling, horse trekking and vehicle travel.

The GPS works by picking up transmissions from orbiting satellites and it will locate your position with great accuracy. Some models include an electronic compass and altimeter, which allow you to predict weather trends and plot your route.

However, like any electronic device the GPS is prone to damage and battery failure, and it should never be carried as an alternative to a conventional map and compass.

to reassure yourself that your course is the correct one. Travelling by compass bearing alone has no second check if things go wrong. Contour line interpretation is the most important skill of navigating and you should aim to regularly "tick off" contour features as you travel. By doing so you maintain a continual check on your position, direction of travel and distance. Then if you do go wrong, you can backtrack to the last point at which you knew you were on the right path, which will not be too far away, and restart from there.

**SETTING A COURSE**

Walking on a compass bearing becomes necessary in poor visibility, at night or on particularly featureless terrain, such as open plains or desert.

To take a compass bearing between two points on a topographical map with grid lines, place the long edge of the protractor base plate along the line between your starting point and your destination. Make sure the direction of travel arrow on the base plate is pointing the right way. Hold the map and compass base plate firmly

▼ *If used correctly a map and compass can help you plan a route, indicate distance and locate your position in the wilderness.*

together. Now turn the protractor around until the lines on the base plate are parallel to the north grid lines on the map. Take the compass off the map and read your grid bearing at the base of the direction of travel arrow. Before you set off on your course you need to apply the local magnetic variation to the bearing. Holding the compass flat in your hand, move yourself around until the red half of the needle is in line with north on the protractor base. Your course is where the direction of travel arrow is now pointing.

### ADJUSTING MAGNETIC NORTH TO TRUE NORTH

The red half of the compass needle points to magnetic north. Your map is drawn to grid north or, with small-scale maps, to true north. In all but very high latitudes the difference between true north and magnetic north is known as magnetic variation. This angle varies dramatically across the globe and, of course, can be easterly or westerly, depending on where you are on earth in relation to the magnetic North Pole.

For compass bearings applied to the ground to be the same as those taken from the map the bearing must be adjusted for magnetic variation. In Europe you will need to add the variation to your grid bearing but in many parts of the world you will need to subtract it. The amount of variation, the direction and the annual change will be printed on your map.

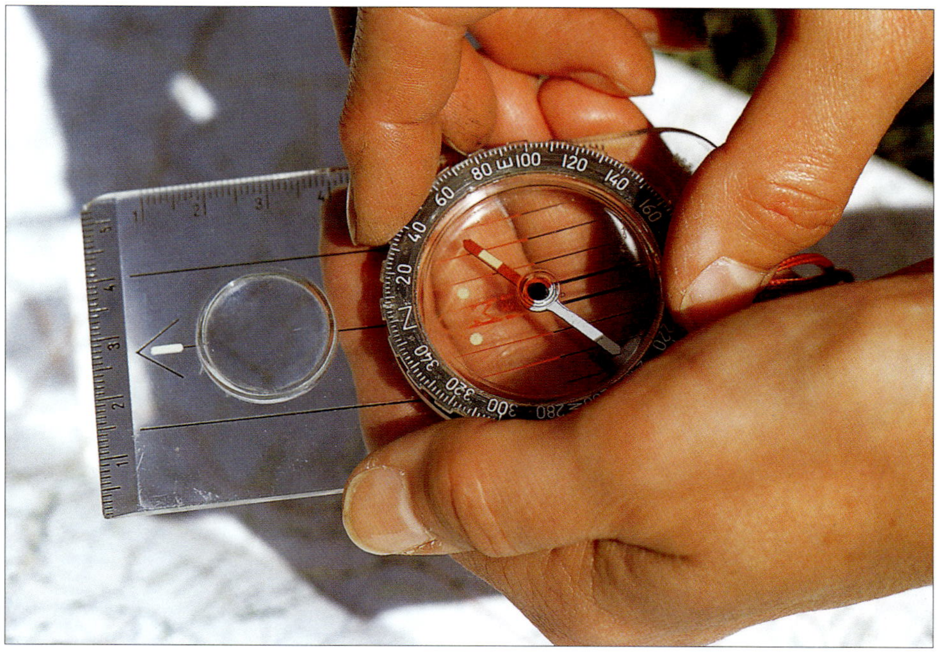

The above information applies if you are taking a bearing off a map and laying it on to the ground (identifying a feature on the ground that falls in the direction of your bearing so that you can use it as a visual guide to your direction). Often you will want to take a bearing off the ground to apply it back to your map – perhaps to check you are on the right route or to locate your position if you have left the route. If you are doing this then the variation needs to be applied in reverse: if when applying information from map to ground you need to add the magnetic variation, then to apply information from ground to map you will need to subtract the variation, and vice versa.

▲ *Magnetic variation needs to be added to, or subtracted from, the grid bearing taken from your map before you try to follow a course using your compass.*

**WILD READINGS**

Whenever you are using a compass, bear in mind that the proximity of large amounts of ferrous metal will affect the accuracy of the reading, giving you what is known as a "wild reading". Far worse, it could permanently damage the compass. Keep any magnetic or iron objects, such as work equipment, well away from the compass at all times.

## SETTING A BEARING USING A MAP AND COMPASS

**1** First connect your start and finish points with the edge of the compass base plate. Make sure the direction of travel arrow is pointing the right way.

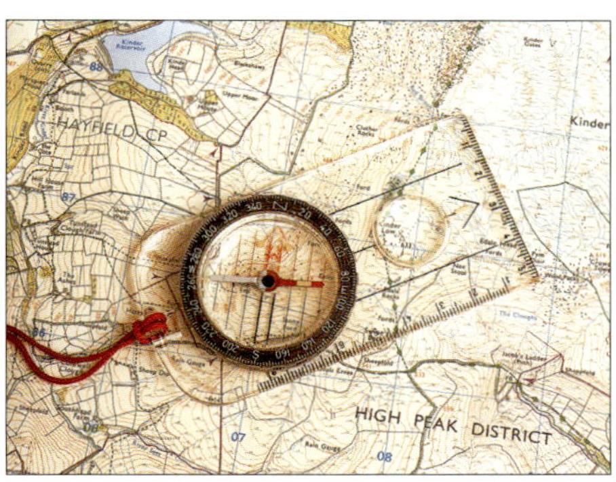


**2** Turn the needle housing around until the lines on the base align with the map grid lines. The arrow on the compass base should point to north on the map.

**3** Add or subtract any magnetic variation. You now have a bearing to walk on as long as the magnetic needle and the direction of travel arrow are aligned.

# Navigation by the Sun, Moon and Stars

Modern man has so many distractions and gadgets that we often fail to notice all the help that nature can give us in finding our way around. There is no doubt that navigating by map and compass is efficient and accurate, but what happens if you are deprived of these tools, if you lose your map or damage your compass?

The heavenly bodies behave in predictable ways, predictions that were worked out by our ancient ancestors and have been used for navigation for centuries. In the event of lost or damaged equipment your ability to use the sun, the moon and the stars to monitor your direction could be a lifesaver, and it pays to commit a few basic principles to memory.

Practise each of the following natural navigation methods before you travel and afterwards use your map and compass to check how you did. Not only will it give you faith in the accuracy of natural signposts, it will also boost your confidence in your own abilities as a navigator. Seasoned navigators are aware of and actively read the signs provided by nature at all times, no matter how sophisticated their modern equipment. After all, the ability to navigate accurately is the most important bushcraft skill of all.

### USING THE SUN

The sun rises in the east and sets in the west every day wherever you are in the world, so you may want to take note of obvious geographical features that are in line with the sunrise or sunset to give you a rough sense of direction for use throughout the day. The techniques outlined below are only useful if the sun is visible, but even with a heavy cloud cover it is usually possible to detect the lightening of the sky that happens at sunrise.This can then be noted for use later in the day.

In the northern hemisphere the sun will be due south at noon and in the southern hemisphere it will be due north. The techniques below are at their most accurate when carried out as near to local noon as possible.

**INACCURATE READINGS**

The nearer you are to the equator the less accurate any attempt to find a direction using the sun will be. When the sun is almost directly overhead it is extremely difficult to determine its direction.

#### Finding north and south using your wristwatch

To do this you will need a traditional analogue watch with two hands set at local time (without variation for summer daylight savings, which do not match real time) and held horizontally. If you are in the northern hemisphere, point the hour hand of your watch towards the sun. Imagine a line halfway between the hour hand and the 12. This line will be pointing roughly south. If you are in the southern hemisphere, point the 12 at the sun and an imaginary line between the 12 and the hour hand will give you a rough indication of north.

### FINDING NORTH AND SOUTH USING A WRISTWATCH

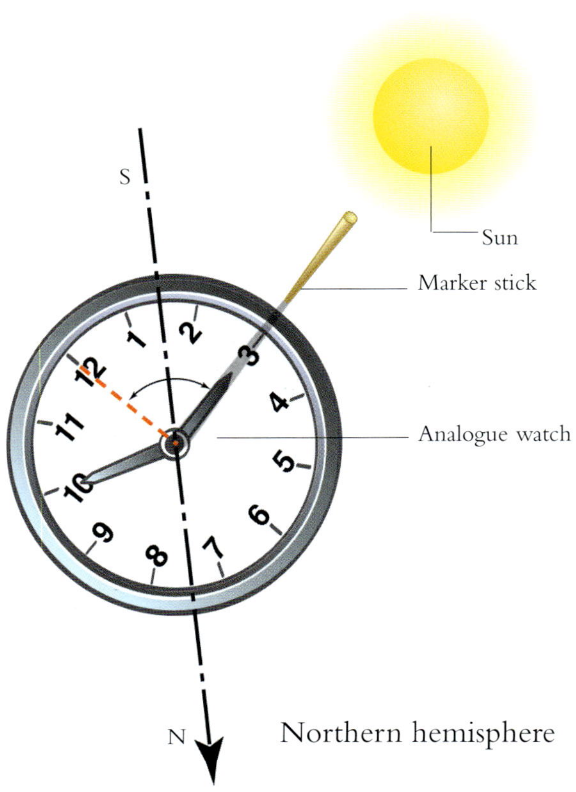


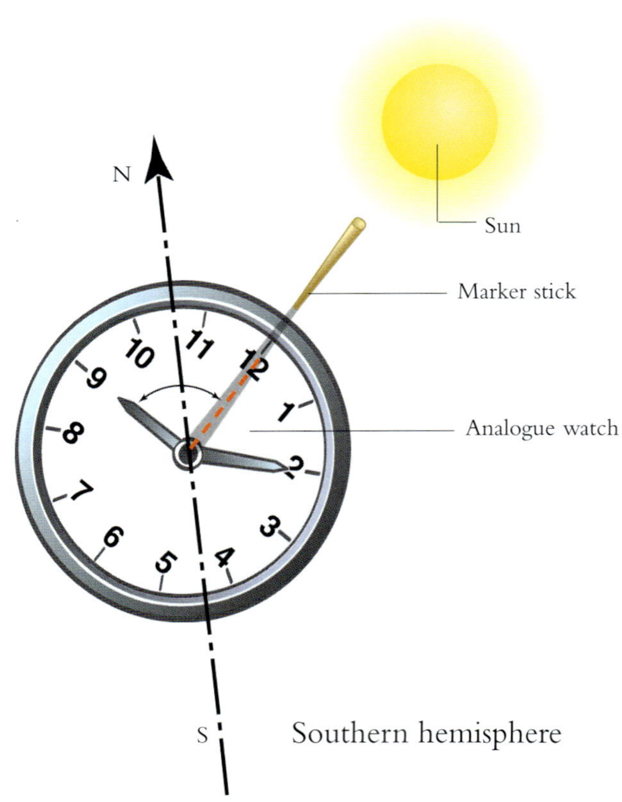

**SEASONAL VARIATION**

It is a well-known fact that the sun rises in the east and sets in the west, but what is less well known is that the sun does not rise and set *exactly* in the east and west. There is some seasonal variation, and you may need to bear this in mind if you need to make decisions based on the general rule.

▲ *Try to be aware of the general direction of the sunrise and sunset at all times, even when you do not need to orienteer yourself.*

### Finding east and west using the shadow stick method

This is a useful method if you are in open country and can afford the time to stop for a while. It works at any time of the day when there is sunshine of any strength, and at any latitude or in either hemisphere.

Select a stick about 90–120cm/3–4ft long and as upright as possible. Plant the stick into a piece of flat ground that is not overlooked by trees, vegetation or any other geological formations. Mark where the tip of the shadow falls with a pebble. Wait for 15–20 minutes and mark where the tip of the new shadow falls, then join the two points together. This line will run east–west with the first point marked being west.

If you will be in your location from the early morning and have time to wait there for almost the entire day, you can try an alternative method using a shadow stick, and the reward is that this is usually more accurate. Plant a stick about 90–120cm/3–4ft long and as upright as possible into the flat, open ground and mark the first shadow tip in the morning. Draw a smooth arc in the ground at exactly this distance from the stick, using the stick as the centre point of the arc. As noon approaches, the shadow will shrink. During the afternoon, the shadow will start to lengthen again, and you need to mark the exact point where it touches the arc. Join up the two points to give an east–west reference, with the mark made in the morning being west.

**WHAT'S IN A SHADOW?**

The way a shadow moves can indicate which hemisphere you are in: clockwise in the northern hemisphere and anticlockwise in the southern hemisphere. A shadow can also be used as a guide to both direction and the time of day.

## SHADOW STICK METHOD

**1** Plant a stick of 90–120cm/3–4ft and as straight as possible into a flat, open piece of ground. Mark the tip of the shadow that forms with a pebble.

**2** Wait for about 15–20 minutes before checking the shadow. It will now have moved, so mark the tip of the new shadow with another pebble.

**3** Lay a stick on the ground to connect the two pebbles. The line that it forms will give you an east–west reference, with the first pebble being west.

► *A moon that is not hidden behind clouds may be able to direct you to reference points for north–south and east–west.*

## USING THE MOON

Unlike the sun the moon has a highly variable pattern of visibility and it is far less bright than the sun. As a result its usefulness as a navigational aid is much more limited, particularly in cloudy conditions when the moon can be almost completely obscured.

The moon reflects the light of the sun and as the moon travels around the earth we see different amounts of its sunlit face, ranging from a sliver crescent through to a full moon. When the moon lies between the sun and the earth the side of the moon facing the earth has no sunlight so we cannot see it at all: this is called a new moon. It takes 29.5 days for the moon to travel round the earth.

If the moon rises before the sun has completely set, the visible side of the moon (which is the side illuminated by the sun) will be on the west. If the moon rises after midnight, when there is no sun, the visible side of the moon will be on the east. A basic rule to remember for an east–west reference at night is that if you can see the moon rising you are facing east, and if you can see it setting you are facing west. This will apply whichever hemisphere you are in.

### Finding north and south using a crescent moon

If the moon is not full, and is not obscured by cloud, you will be able to work out a simple north or south reference during the night. Looking up at the moon, imagine a line drawn through the two tips of the crescent moon and continue the line all the way down to the horizon. If the two tips of the crescent are on the left, the point where the imaginary line meets the horizon will be roughly south in the northern hemisphere and roughly north in the southern hemisphere. If the tips of the crescent are on the right the reverse is true, and the point at which the imaginary line meets the horizon will indicate north in the northern hemisphere and south in the southern hemisphere.

▼ *The diagram below shows how to find north or south using a crescent moon. The dotted line connects the tips of the left-hand moon and meets the horizon at a point that is south in the northern hemisphere and north in the southern hemisphere. The right-hand moon shows the other way a crescent moon can appear. Here, the dotted line intersects the horizon at north in the northern hemisphere and south in the southern hemisphere.*

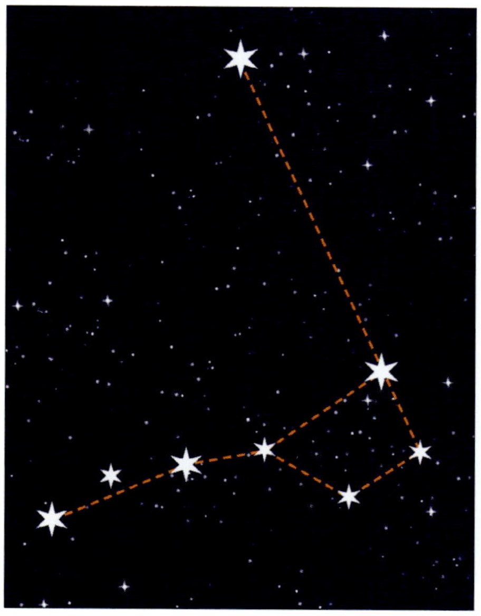

▲ *The North Star lies above the North Pole and can be found by running a line into the sky from the far side of the Plough's pan.*

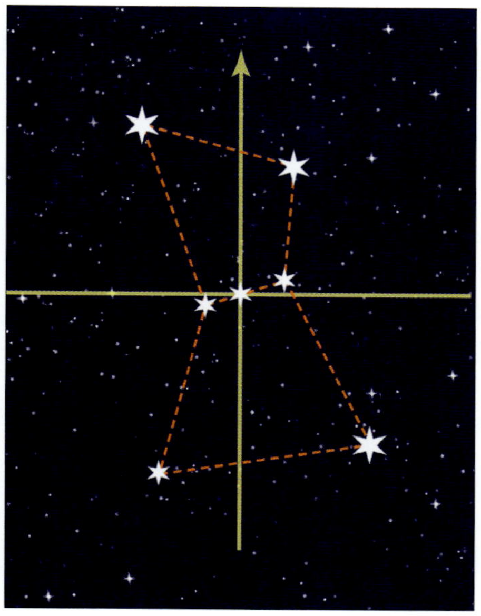

▲ *An imaginary line drawn across the middle of the Orion constellation lies roughly east–west in the northern hemisphere.*

▲ *The Southern Cross will help you to find south in the southern hemisphere. Note the false cross of dimmer stars to the right.*

## USING THE STARS

Because of the many and varied constellations, navigation by the stars is by far the most complex part of celestial navigation and therefore the most difficult to commit to memory. The constellations and individual stars visible from the two hemispheres differ, and this adds to the difficulty. Despite this, stars have been used for navigation for tens of thousands of years.

As the earth is constantly moving, note that the star constellations may appear upside down or sideways when compared to the above diagrams. Like the sun, star constellations always rise in the east and set in the west.

### In the northern hemisphere

To find north, locate the North Star or Polaris, which lies over the North Pole. This is one of the brightest stars in the sky and the only one that appears to remain static. To locate it, first find the pan-shaped constellation known as the Plough or Big Dipper. Follow the two stars that form the far side of the pan for six times the distance between them; this will bring you to the North Star.

To find an east–west line, use the star constellation known as Orion or the Hunter. A line taken through the three stars that make up the Hunter's belt lies roughly east–west.

### In the southern hemisphere

The North Star is not visible in the southern hemisphere and there is no equivalent star coveniently lying over the South Pole. Instead you can use the Southern Cross constellation. To find it, look towards the middle of the Milky Way where there is a dark area known as the Coal Sack. Straddling this area is the Southern Cross: four bright stars forming a cross plus a fifth fainter star and two bright pointer stars. (A false cross of dimmer stars lies to the right.) Follow the longest line through the cross and down four-and-a-half times its length, then look down to the horizon and that will be due south.

#### NAVIGATIONAL STARS

**North Star** Also known as Polaris and the Pole Star. Located above the North Pole it is a key reference for north. It is the only star that remains static; all other stars move around it.
**The Plough** Also known as the Big Dipper. It forms part of the large Great Bear star constellation.
**Orion** Also known as the Hunter. This rises above the Equator and can be seen in both hemispheres.
**Milky Way** A hazy band of millions of stars that stretches across the sky. In the middle of it is the Coal Sack.

#### MARKING YOUR DIRECTION

When using the moon and stars as navigational tools, do not forget that they will not be visible the next day when the sun has risen. If you are not planning to start on your course straight away during the night, you will need to mark the direction to give yourself a reference point for the morning. Mark your course with a stick or identify it with a prominent object on the horizon, so that you will know which way to go without your guiding moon and stars.

▲ *Remember to mark the direction with a stick or a pebble before daylight breaks.*

# Other Natural Signposts

Nature provides us with endless clues to help us establish direction, which we can gather from the physical, animal and plant worlds. Natural signs will only provide an approximate direction and you may soon leave behind or lose the clue that is helping you, but if all else is unavailable you may be very grateful that you took the time to digest the following points. Ideally, you should hunt for a combination of signs to determine your direction.

**THE WIND**

Many parts of the world have consistent wind patterns where the prevailing wind will blow in the same direction for the whole year or part of the year. If you are able to find out this information in advance, you may be able to use the wind as an aid to orientation. Beware of the effect that land formations have on wind. For example, deep valleys or steep ridges can completely change true wind direction. The only accurate way to establish true wind direction is to look at the clouds in the free air.

Trees and bushes in exposed places will lean away from and be shaped by the prevailing wind. However, in some areas of the tropics palm trees will grow into the wind; this goes against the general rule but the palm trees will still give an indication of wind direction.

The wind also leaves clues in sand and snow. Sand and snow drifts always form downwind of any obstruction.

▲ *Find out about the direction of prevailing winds in the area you are travelling to: local people will often be able to tell you.*

▼ *Trees in an open landscape can help you determine the wind direction, but by far the most accurate guide is the clouds up above.*

▼ *Never trust the wind direction in steep valleys or canyons as land formations can have a severe effect on how the wind blows.*

Wind blows up the sloping side of the drift before meeting the obstruction that causes it to deposit its load of sand or snow. So, from the direction the drift faces you can deduce which way the wind was blowing when it was formed.

### VEGETATION

Plants need sunlight and water to survive, and analysing where and how well they are growing can help us to establish our direction. Because of the interplay between sun and water, you may have to think about which influences are the more dominant, depending on whether you are in a hot, dry country or cold, wet country. Mosses and lichens dry out quickly, and will generally grow on the cooler, damper sides of trees or rocks, away from the sun. In cold areas, larger plants and trees will dominate the warm sides of terrain and most plants will grow more prolifically on the sunward side. Having sorted this out think about which hemisphere you are in. Some plants, such as the North Pole Plant, which grows in South Africa, will lean to the north to take advantage of the sun. Many flowers move from east to west on a daily basis, following the sun as it moves across the sky.

▼ *Moss will grow on the northern side of trees in the northern hemisphere, and on the southern side in the southern hemisphere.*

▲ *Snowfall at the base of trees can show the direction of the prevailing wind, and you may be able to use this for navigation.*

### SNOWY TERRAIN

If you are in or can see snow-covered terrain you will see that the snow cover is more extensive on land sheltered from the sun. Likewise, snow will be markedly deeper on land to the lee of the prevailing wind. It will depend on where you are as to which direction you can establish from these observations. You may already know whether or not the prevailing wind blows in the same direction year-round. If so, and you can establish the wind direction, you can orienteer yourself accordingly.

**WARNING**

Natural signposts are useful aids to navigation, but the information they give is only approximate, and you should look for a variety of signs and make a careful assessment before making important decisions.

### ANIMAL TRACKS

In dry country, if you see animal tracks following in one direction, it is likely they will be heading for a water source. This can also be true of flocks of birds, though the distances can be far greater. In very heavy vegetation, animal tracks can help in making headway and will often lead to more open country, which may allow you more visibility to plan your subsequent route.

### ANT HILLS

In Australia, ants and termites build their nests in the form of mounds or thin blade-like structures. These are always orientated north–south, so that they can take full advantage of the sun's warmth in both the morning and the afternoon in winter; in the summer months the ant hill structures offer some shade from the intense sun.

▼ *Wildlife can be a very valuable source of information. Animal tracks on the ground may be able to lead you to a water source.*

# Understanding the Weather

When planning a trip, the weather can be of vital importance, so it is sensible to learn what all the terms and symbols shown on a weather map and referred to on a radio forecast mean. Knowing the highest and lowest temperatures for the area you are travelling to, and the expected rainfall for each month, is also very useful.

**ISOBARS**

Meteorologists measure the atmospheric pressure at internationally agreed times, every three hours. After plotting these readings on maps, they draw lines known as isobars, which link places of equal pressure.

The closer these lines are to each other, the higher the wind speed will be, because they show that the pressure values are changing quickly over a relatively small area. The isobars on a chart form the shapes of concentric rings which indicate areas of low pressure (depressions or cyclones) and high pressure (anticyclones).

▼ *Low-pressure areas, indicated by closely spaced concentric circles of isobars, are often associated with warm or cold fronts.*

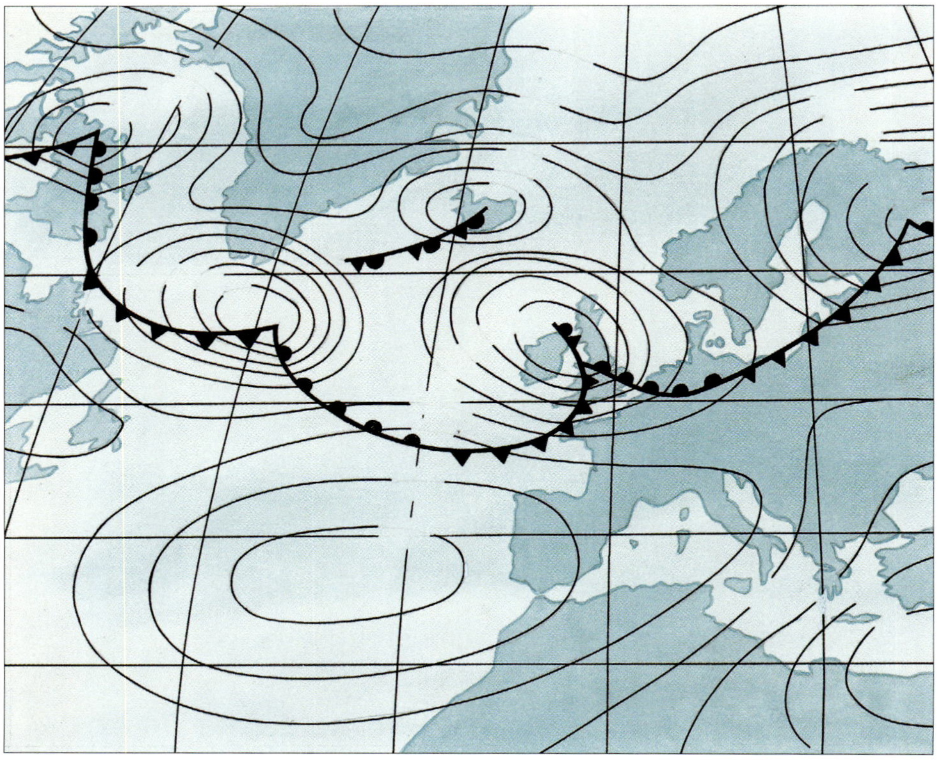

**FRONTS**

A weather front is marked as a heavy line on the chart, with either small triangles (a cold front) or semicircles (a warm front) on it. A front marks the edges of air masses of different origins and at different temperatures.

A warm front indicates that warm air is advancing and rising over cold air. This usually leads to a bout of heavy rain, followed by a rise in temperature. A cold front shows that cold air is replacing warm air at ground level. This leads to a short spell of heavy rain followed by much brighter weather with showers and gusty winds.

**DEPRESSIONS**

These may be described as low-pressure areas or cyclones in the northern hemisphere. When pressure falls, the winds blow in an anticlockwise direction (clockwise in the southern hemisphere), often bringing rain.

**ANTICYCLONES, OR HIGHS**

In anticyclones, winds blow clockwise in the northern and anticlockwise in the southern hemispheres. They are indicated on a weather chart by areas of widely spaced isobars. The pressure is high and the winds are light. Highs bring sunny weather in summer, cold and foggy conditions in winter.

▲ *In an anticyclone, air is descending, compressing and warming. Clouds tend to evaporate and winds are generally light.*

▼ *In a depression, air is rising, expanding and cooling. Water vapour condenses, forming clouds and leading to rain or snow.*

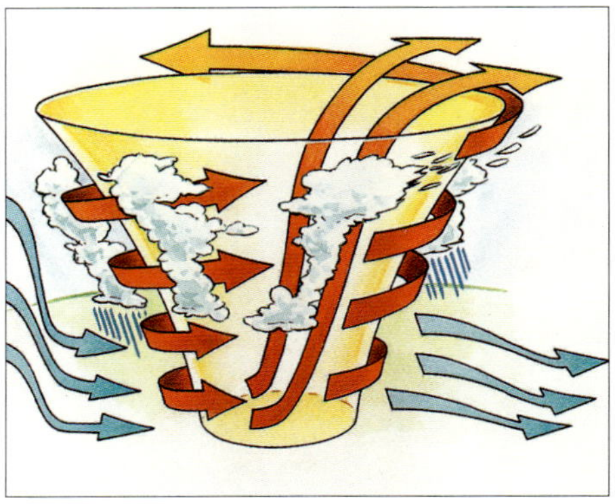

**WIND**

The speed of winds is measured in knots, but a system called the Beaufort scale is also used to describe the kind of wind indicated by the wind speed.

Regarding wind temperature, as a general rule, summer winds that have come over a landmass will be warmer and drier than those that have come over the sea. In winter, winds that have travelled over a large landmass will be colder than those that have travelled over the sea. In the northern hemisphere, winds from the north will be colder than those from the south, and in the southern hemisphere the reverse is true.

▲ *Cirrocumulus clouds signify a blue sky and fair weather. They often follow a storm.*

▲ *Altocumulus clouds predict fair weather. They will often follow a storm shower.*

▲ *Cumulus clouds indicate fair weather if widely separated; they may produce showers.*

▲ *Stratocumulus clouds covering the sky mean light showers which dissipate quickly.*

▲ *Heavy rain or snow is signified by the dark low cloud cover known as nimbostratus.*

▲ *Stratus clouds look like hill fog. Although not a rain cloud they can produce drizzle.*

**BEAUFORT SCALE OF WIND FORCE**

| Beaufort number | General description | Sea criterion | Landsman's criterion | Velocity in knots |
|---|---|---|---|---|
| 0 | Calm | Sea like a mirror | Calm; smoke rises vertically | Less than 1 |
| 1 | Light air | Ripples with appearance of scales form but without foam crests | Direction of wind shown by smoke drift but not wind vanes | 1–3 |
| 2 | Light breeze | Small wavelets, short but pronounced; crests look glassy and do not break | Wind felt on face; leaves rustle; ordinary vanes moved by wind | 4–6 |
| 3 | Gentle breeze | Large wavelets; crests begin to break; foam of glassy appearance; scattered white horses | Leaves and small twigs in constant motion; wind extends light flags | 7–10 |
| 4 | Moderate breeze | Small waves become longer; fairly frequent white horses | Raises dust and loose paper; small branches are moved | 11–16 |
| 5 | Fresh breeze | Moderate waves take pronounced form; many white horses; chance of spray | Small trees in leaf begin to sway; crested wavelets form on inland waters | 17–21 |
| 6 | Strong breeze | Large waves form; white foam crests more extensive; probably spray | Large branches in motion; whistling in telegraph wires; umbrellas used with difficulty | 22–27 |
| 7 | Near gale | Sea heaps up and white foam from breaking waves is blown in streaks in direction of wind | Whole trees in motion; inconvenience felt when walking against wind | 28–33 |
| 8 | Gale | Moderately high waves of greater length; edges of crests break into spindrift; foam is blown in well-marked streaks | Breaks twigs off trees; impedes progress when walking | 34–40 |
| 9 | Strong gale | High waves; dense streaks of foam along direction of wind; wave crests topple; spray may affect visibility | Slight structural damage (chimney pots and slates removed) | 41–47 |
| 10 | Storm | Very high waves with long overhanging crests; foam in great patches is blown in dense streaks along wind direction; surface takes on white appearance; visibility affected | Trees uprooted; considerable structural damage occurs | 48–55 |

# Hot Weather

A basic understanding of the weather is invaluable when you are pursuing any kind of outdoor activity, but you also need to know what to do in extreme environmental conditions. It is not always obvious how to respond to extreme heat and humidity, or to lightning, and many people end up endangering themselves by doing the wrong thing.

In many hot countries, all the weather is extreme. When it rains, very large amounts of water can be deposited in a short space of time. When the wind blows, it is with destructive force. Of course the sun can burn your skin in a short time, even (in fact sometimes especially) on overcast days.

You must always remember that in some places there are large temperature variations. Maritime climates (that is, in places near the sea) can have a fairly constant temperature day and night. In contrast, in the central areas of large continents the temperature may be 40°C/104°F or higher in the daytime but drop below 0°C/32°F at night.

▲ *A cyclone is a funnel of whirling wind that produces extremely low pressure at its base, which acts like a giant vacuum cleaner.*

**SUN**

Prolonged exposure to the sun in any climate will lead you to suffer from sunburn, especially at high altitude or in the tropics or in ozone depleted regions like the Antarctic on the tip of South America. Wear appropriate clothing, sunscreen and/or sunblock to protect your skin. The short-term effects of sunburn can be painful, and the long-term ones fatal, so you must simply not allow it to happen.

**HYDRATION**

In a hot and humid environment, such as a rainforest or during a monsoon season, your biggest danger is heatstroke and/or dehydration, although you may be surrounded by water. You will be perspiring at the maximum rate possible for your body, but the perspiration will not evaporate from your skin in the 100 per cent humidity. This means that your body does not cool down, so it continues to sweat as much as it can to try to achieve this. But it makes no difference to your temperature and you lose water at an incredible rate. All you can do in this situation is keep drinking the coldest water you can safely use, to keep hydrated and try to reduce your core temperature.

**STORMS**

You should find out about and understand any predictable local weather conditions. In hot climates, storms often occur nearly every day as the land heats up, and you should take care not to be caught out. Especially avoid being on the water in a boat, whether travelling by canoe on a lake, or at sea. If you are caught by a storm while afloat, tie everything down and try to keep the centre of gravity of the boat as low as possible. In the event of a wreck or capsize, try to stay with your craft if you can.

You can often predict the onset of electrical storms by the presence of cumulonimbus and anvil clouds, often massing together. Beware if you find yourself downwind of these cloud formations – this means the storm is coming your way. Storms triggered by heat tend to hit in the afternoon or early evening, but they can happen at any time. Such storms often bring with them heavy rain or hailstones.

Even if lightning is not hitting the ground and endangering personnel, you should be aware that electrical activity in a storm can damage navigation gear such as GPS, and knock out communications equipment, so this could endanger your party.

### Lightning

If you are out in the open space of a desert or savanna, a lightning storm can be very impressive but it is also very dangerous. If the lightning is very close and you feel you are in danger of being struck, crouch down, with your head as low as possible, and put your hands over your head.

You are in more danger from lightning if you are near trees or any upward pointing object. You are also in great danger if you are on water. Surprisingly, however, on land you are safer in the open, as long as you curl up as described. One of the safest places to be is in a car.

### Bushfires

Lightning is frequently the cause of bushfires. If one starts near you, or is coming towards you, and you cannot get out of the way, find an open space and consider burning your own firebreak, but remember that fire can jump quite large distances. If you have to escape a fire, remember that it travels upwards: rather than going up to a ridge, stay down in a valley.

Be warned that the fire will flush out all sorts of animal life, so be careful of snakes and larger animals being forced out to share your space. If the fire is near your camp, make sure you get well away from all gas canisters and similar inflammable materials.

### Hurricanes, tornadoes and typhoons

There is little you can do in the face of storms of this magnitude, except to hide from them. Don't stay inside a building that could be destroyed by the storm. The best protection is a safe basement of a very solid construction.

### Dust and sandstorms

Desert areas are normally windy places, but if the wind becomes strong enough, it starts picking up first the surface dust and then, as it gets stronger, particles of sand. These storms can last from a few hours to a number of days, and if you are caught in one you can become disoriented. In any area where you are going to encounter blowing sand and dust, make sure your eyes and ears are protected with goggles and maybe a headscarf or headdress.

Driving can become very dangerous, as you will be disoriented and unable to see where you are driving. You should stop and park the vehicle with the engine facing away from the prevailing wind. Close all heating/air-conditioning vents to stop the sand being drawn inside the vehicle.

If you are with animals, turn their backs to the wind while you sit out the storm. Camels should sit down, but horses, mules and donkeys will stand.

▼ *If lightning is striking the ground near you during a storm, don't be tempted to shelter under trees as they may be struck.*

## SEASONAL EFFECTS

Many tropical countries have very distinct wet and dry seasons, and transport and logistics may be affected in the wet season due to roads and bridges being washed away, and routes blocked by landslides.

### Rain

A violent downpour on dry, baked land may have effects some 36–54km/20–30 miles away. The rain will run off into a dried-up river system that may have been dry for many months, and can turn it into a raging torrent in just a few hours.

This can be very dangerous if you are camped or are walking in a dried-up watercourse. It may be that no rain has fallen where you are and you will therefore not expect a flood.

### Mud and landslides

Landslides may be the result of heavy rain and they can be even more destructive than a flood. If it is still raining, never try to walk or drive through one, since where one slide has happened, another can follow.

# Cold Weather

▲ *Fast-falling snow quickly transforms the landscape, and if it is combined with a high wind, deep drifts can soon build up.*

If you are travelling in or to countries where the temperature rarely rises above freezing, such as those in polar regions at any time, at high altitude, or inshore in very large continents during the winter, you must know how to survive in blizzards, avoid avalanches, and move safely across snow and ice.

Intense cold can damage the lining of the lungs, so always cover your nose and mouth and breathe through a scarf or something similar so that the air is slightly warmed before you inhale it. You are also in danger from hypothermia and frostbite, so make sure all your clothing and equipment is up to scratch.

**BLIZZARDS**

In a blizzard, heavy snow is accompanied by strong winds. In extreme cases, the driven snow fills the air and can reduce visibility to less than a metre/yard. It can also cause drifting and very quickly build up large drifts, which can close roads and even cover tents or buildings.

If you are caught in a blizzard, always seek shelter and be prepared to sit it out, even though this may take several days. If you are inside a tent when the blizzard strikes, you may have to dig your tent out occasionally to stop the weight of snow from collapsing it. Also, make sure the snow is not blocking up your ventilation, as people have suffocated in tents or snow holes when the snow has blocked the door or ventilation holes.

**AVALANCHES**

There are two main types of avalanche: powder snow and slab. Powder snow avalanches usually consist of newly fallen snow and can be very destructive, mowing down whole forests and villages. Slab avalanches are particularly liable to fall in the spring melt. They move more slowly at the edges and the base than in the centre. They also can be very destructive and their weight can crush anything in their path.

Before you visit a cold country, you should find out if the area is prone to avalanches and know what signs to look for that will tell you when there is a high risk of one occurring. These include rapid snowfall, leading to a buildup of more than 30cm/12in new snow, and sudden rises in temperature.

**ICE**

Be cautious when approaching any expanse of frozen water, as the ice can be anything from 1m/1yd to only a few centimetres/inches thick. If anyone does fall through the ice, they must be got out as soon as possible and treated for hypothermia (see the section Cold-weather Effects). Anybody going to the person's rescue should beware of becoming another casualty.

Remember that thin ice could be covered by snow. When this is possible you will have to make slow careful progress, checking as you go. Walking on skis or snowshoes can reduce your likelihood of breaking the ice.

If you are on steep ground and start to encounter ice, and cannot avoid it, put on a pair of crampons if you have them. If not, pull a spare pair of socks over your boots, which will give more grip than ordinary soles.

Ice can be a hazard for travellers in vehicles as well as on foot. The ice you can see on a road or track is not your greatest problem, however: it is the ice that may be hidden under a light covering of snow or slush that will cause the accident.

▼ *Navigation can be much more difficult when you are travelling through a snowy landscape where visible landmarks are few.*

**ALTITUDE**

As you gain altitude the air becomes colder. This is because the air pressure is less, and so the air is less compressed. On a clear day the temperature might typically decrease by 1°C/2°F per 100m/330ft of altitude. If you are under or in cloud, this fall might be reduced to about 0.5°C/1°F as a result of the heat that is released by the condensation process.

**TEMPERATURE INVERSION**

This usually occurs after a clear night in the mountains. The mountain tops become very cold, and this cools the air in contact with them. The air is now heavy, and rolls down the mountain to make the valleys very cold, forcing the warm air of the valley back up the mountains.

**SUNBURN**

Even in a cold climate prolonged exposure can result in sunburn, especially in ozone-depleted regions such as the Antarctic on the tip of South America, and you should take all usual precautions to protect your skin.

► *It is dangerous to approach an iceberg: a boat may be capsized by turbulence if the berg moves, or underwater ice may ram it.*

▼ *Thick snow may mask watercourses, but you should take extreme care when crossing ice in case you fall through and get wet.*

**WIND CHILL**

Inanimate objects, including thermometers, are not affected by wind chill, so although a thermometer may accurately measure the air temperature, the combined effect of the temperature and the prevailing wind may have a serious effect on the human body, leading to conditions such as hypothermia and frostbite.

Wearing layers of clothing helps to insulate the body, trapping layers of warm air, while cutting down the penetration of the wind and preventing it carrying away heat.

# Signalling

Before you embark on any expedition you must consider how you will get help should an emergency arise. You should make sure that others know your plans and route, so that they can take action if you do not return, but if you are ill, injured, lost or stranded in some way you may need to be able to signal to your potential rescuers.

There are two types of distress signal: those that use specialized equipment and those that rely on natural materials. If you are spending time in wild areas, you will find it useful to understand and be able to use both types in case you need them.

If you are going to a national park or wilderness area, you should find out in advance if there is any special system of distress signals that you need to use there, and make sure you and the rest of your party learn it. Alternatively, you may be required to carry a certain amount of specialized survival equipment while you are in the area, and this is likely to include any relevant signalling equipment.

▲ *A rescue helicopter may need to make a difficult or dangerous landing to reach you, so your signals to the crew must be clear.*

**BASIC DISTRESS SIGNALS**

If you need help you must be able to convey a message that anyone who sees it will understand. "SOS" (short for "Save Our Souls") is an internationally recognized distress signal. It may be transmitted using Morse code (three dots, three dashes and three dots) by the flashes of a mirror or flashlight, or by smoke signals, or it could be written on the ground as a visual message. The radio call "mayday" (from the French "m'aider") is understood worldwide.

You can also learn the international mountain distress signal, which consists of six flashes of a flashlight, six blasts on a whistle, or waving something for one minute, followed by a minute's silence. The signal is then repeated. The reply from anyone who sees it is three flashes, blasts or waves.

All these signals are taken seriously and you should use them only when you are in trouble.

**VISUAL AND AUDIO SIGNALS**

If rescue is likely to be coming in the form of a helicopter or plane, you will need to rig up a visual signal that is large enough to attract the attention of the crew. If your rescuers are likely to arrive by land, an audio signal, such as a whistle, will be more effective.

Obviously, any visual ground signals you decide to use must be arranged on sites in open ground, where they can be clearly seen from any direction. You will also need to set up different signals by day and by night, whereas audio signals are equally effective in daylight and darkness.

If you are in a vehicle of some kind, you should always stay with it, as it will offer you some shelter from the elements and you may need to protect yourself from wild animals, particularly at night. A vehicle is also a visual signal in its own right, as it is reasonably large and can be seen from the air, especially if you put bright objects on its roof and beside it. Finally, if you have told people which route you were planning to take, a rescue party will follow it when looking for you.

**WHISTLES**

Everybody in the party should carry a whistle at all times and should know the international mountain distress signal or any special signals you may

◀ *If you need to make a visual signal, choose an open area where you have a good chance of being seen from land and air.*

▲ *A bright orange bivvy bag can be spread out to make a ground marker.*

▲ *A folded space blanket can be used to catch the sun's rays and flash an SOS signal.*

► *If you take a mobile phone, make sure you load it with all the relevant numbers, but you should use them only in a real emergency and not abuse the goodwill of the rescue services.*

have decided on. They are not only useful for attracting the attention of a rescue party, but can be used by any member of the expedition who strays off the path and gets lost.

## MOBILE PHONES

In some countries you may be able to use a mobile (cellular) phone to make contact with the rescue services if an emergency situation arises. This can be a vital timesaver in cases of injury or sudden illness, though its availability should never lead you to lower your usual standards of safety precautions and the correct equipment.

You will need to know in advance the right numbers to call for help or rescue, though some spectacular rescues have been achieved when climbers in difficulty have phoned home to get relatives to contact the rescue services on their behalf.

## PERSONAL EQUIPMENT

If you are in dense scrub or forest, lay your equipment out in a long line on either side of your position, so people looking for you on the ground will have more chance of finding you. Items of equipment can also be laid out on the ground in an open situation to form a visual signal to show an air crew your position.

## SPECIAL SIGNALLING EQUIPMENT

A range of emergency equipment is available to help with signalling. You will probably not want to, or be able to, carry all these methods with you, so you need to decide which would be best for your situation.

### Transmitters and rescue beacons

This traditional marine method of signalling is becoming far more common for use on land, but the transmitters can have a limited range and are reliant on batteries. Before you go into the wilds, arrange two times in the day when you will transmit if you are in trouble – say midday and midnight – then simply transmit for around 15 minutes at both of these times to give the recipients time to pinpoint your position.

▲ *A stand allows a flashlight or strobe light to be set up for signalling.*

► *Carrying a flashlight will allow you to send the international mountain distress signal.*

### Flashlight and strobe lights

A flashlight will allow you to flash a signal or to guide your rescuers to you. Once you switch on a strobe light, it will give a bright flash several times a minute and can be seen at night over great distances.

▼ *Strobe lights can be seen over long distances if they are placed in positions of good visibility.*

◄ *A strobe light fitted with an adjustable strap can be fixed to a cycle frame or hoisted on a pole.*

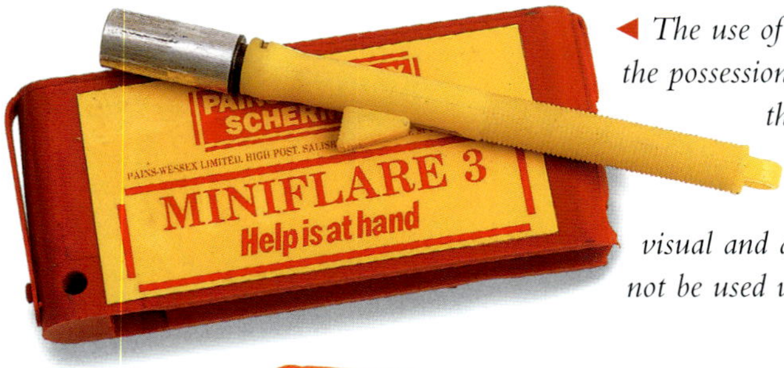


◀ *The use of some types of flares requires the possession of a firearms licence, and they can be dangerous.*

▼ *Flares provide both a visual and an audio signal but should not be used without proper training.*

### Flares and smoke

These can be bought from specialized stores and ships' chandlers. Some may require a firearms certificate. Flares give both a visual and an audio signal, but they can be dangerous and need to be handled with great care, following the instructions that come with them. You should not let anyone handle them who has not been trained in their use.

Flare and smoke containers will become very hot during use, so wear gloves if possible when you are holding them.

Smoke is useful as a visual signal to attract help from the air or on the ground, though for ground rescue it will need to be on an exposed site that can be seen from a distance. If you do not have smoke containers with you, you can of course light a fire to create a plume of smoke.

▲ *Tilt the reflector so that the sunlight shines on the plane, and keep it moving to attract the attention of the pilot.*

### Heliographs

A heliograph is a flat, shiny plate, usually silver-coloured, that uses light reflected from the sun to send a flashing light signal. A hole in the middle will help you to direct the sun's rays to the place you are trying to signal to. Heliograph signals can be seen from a great distance. They are quick and require little energy. However, they do need bright, sunny conditions.

By holding the heliograph in the direction of the sun and tilting it

▼ *A heliograph is a good way of attracting the attention of a pilot too far away to see you, as it is visible over a long distance.*

### GROUND-TO-AIR CODE

This international code is designed to be laid out on the ground, using special panels or any natural materials you can find, such as branches, rocks or pebbles. You could also draw the symbols in sand or mud. Make them as large as you can so they can be seen clearly and interpreted correctly.

Some of the messages are particularly useful if you need supplies to be dropped but do not need rescuing, because they allow a plane or helicopter crew to decipher your needs without having to make a risky landing.

Serious injury – immediate

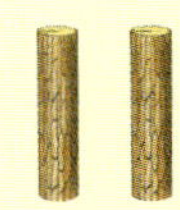

Need medical supplies

Need food

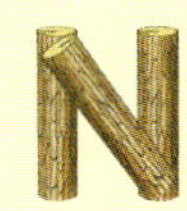

Negative

Affirmative

All is well

Unable to

Am moving

Show direction

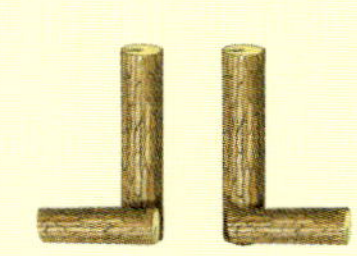

Do not

Need compass and map

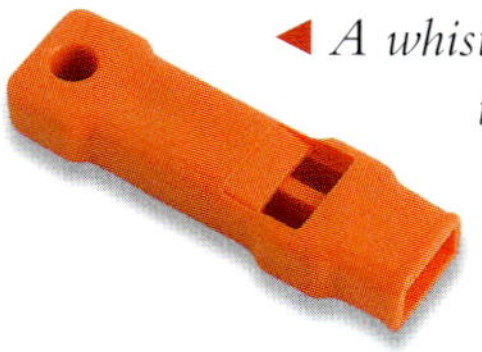

▲ *A whistle should be part of the basic survival kit of every member of the expedition.*

downwards until the beam of sunlight hits the ground you can make sure you have it in the correct position. Move the panel to flash the light upwards to a passing aircraft or a distant position where a rescuer might spot it.

### Water dye

If you are in a boat and need to send a distress signal, a water dye pack can be seen as soon as it is released into the water. The intense colour of the dye patch makes it highly visible, and it can be seen by air rescue more easily than a small boat.

Dye is a very effective way to mark your position on still water, such as on a lake. It is less effective on the sea, where the movement of the waves quickly causes the dye to dissipate and disperse.

### Ground-to-air signal panels

Usually made of material in fluorescent colours, these panels can be laid out on the ground as a ground-to-air signal or on a hillside as a ground-to-ground signal. They should measure at least 180 x 75cm/6ft x 2½ft. They can be used to lay out the international ground-to-air code, which it is useful to know (see box).

## NATURAL SIGNALS

If you are ill-prepared, or just unlucky, you may not have any specialized method of signalling to hand. You can, however, indicate your position by forming an "SOS" on the ground, or by marking out the relevant ground-to-air signal using part of your kit or any natural materials you can find, such as branches or stones.

You can dig or scrape "SOS" in the earth or snow, or in the sand on a beach. Make the letters as large as you can and build up the sides so that during the day the shadows cast will help the letters to stand out. On snow, you may be able to fill the base of the letters with wood, rocks or earth so that they will be clearer. If you have fuel from a vehicle, sprinkle some of it along the letters and then light it at night if you hear a plane overhead.

If you use this kind of signal, make sure it is destroyed when you are rescued or if you move away, otherwise other rescuers may see it and endanger their own lives trying to find a non-existent survivor.

## FIRES

A fire makes a good signal at night, and if you place boughs of fresh green foliage over the flames during the day it will produce dense smoke, which will make an effective signal both to the air and on the ground. Even if you are not using a fire to keep warm, you should have it prepared in advance, with plenty of fuel ready, so that you can light it quickly if you hear or see possible rescue coming.

▲ *Have a fire ready to light if you hear rescuers coming, with some green foliage ready to put on it to create smoke.*

▼ *In misty conditions a smoke signal may not be seen, and you will not be able to reflect the sun, but a flashlight may work.*

# TRAVELLING

**The wilderness areas of the world survive because they present a challenge to the traveller, whether of extremes of climate, ruggedness of terrain, lack of water or sheer distance from today's human settlements. Time moves at a different pace in such places, and to appreciate the wonders they offer we need to match that pace by travelling slowly – on foot, with animals or by pedal or paddle power.**

# Planning your Day's Travel

Before the journey begins you will have planned your overall route and, unless you are wilderness camping, will probably be aiming for specific locations for overnight stops. However, unforeseen events, particularly changing weather conditions, often mean that you need to establish the details of the route on a daily basis.

▲ *When travelling by water, your daily route planning needs to take into account suitable landing and launch points as well as the distance you can paddle.*

**DISTANCE**

Always plan to start your trip with a relatively short day, mileage-wise, and gradually build up to longer distances each day as you get used to carrying a full pack. Factor in either an easy day or a rest day every four to six days.

When planning a long-distance walk, most people tend to overestimate how far they can go. Most fit and experienced walkers will enjoy walking 16–24km/10–15 miles a day, though much will depend on the kind of terrain you are covering, and the weather conditions you can expect. If you will be carrying your cooking and camping equipment, then you should expect to achieve no more than 16km/10 miles a day, or even 13km/8 miles a day to begin with.

The appropriate distance for a day's travelling can vary even more when your journey is by bicycle, kayak or canoe, or with animals or a vehicle. As with walking, much will depend on your level of experience, and on the terrain and climate.

**REST DAYS**

Don't forget to rest during your journey. If you are exploring a new area it's easy to feel that a day not travelling is a wasted day. However, if you are moving under your own steam your body will rebel if you don't give it an adequate break from time to time.

In a group, individual members' needs for rest will vary, and the timing of rest days may depend on where you are: it makes sense to organize prolonged stops at interesting sights or in beautiful surroundings where everyone will be content to linger.

**WATER AND FOOD**

An adequate supply of drinking water should be your first consideration. Establish whether water will be available at your campsites and along the route. This does not have to be drinking water, it could be water from rivers or streams that you can purify yourself for drinking and cooking. On mountains or in polar regions snow can be melted for water. On parts of your route where water will not be available, you will have to carry your own supplies. Top up your water containers whenever you have the opportunity. As you will be active, each person in the group should expect to drink at least 4 litres/7 pints of water per day, or as much as 8 litres/14 pints in hot weather. Don't be tempted to carry sweetened or alcoholic drinks with you: they will

► *Fill your water bottle before you leave camp; if you have to refill the bottle use a water purifier.*

▲ *In mountains, where clouds come and go, always take the opportunity of checking your route when you get a clear spell.*

▲ *When packing your bicycle, always arrange the load carefully so that it can be controlled safely.*

simply increase your need for water and could even lead to dehydration if your water supply is limited.

A substantial breakfast and evening meal, and a high-energy snack at midday, are the best combination on days when you will be active and away from camp during the day. Apart from adding to the weight of your pack, too much food in the middle of the day will make you feel sluggish in the afternoon while you digest your lunch. Choose trail snacks carefully: unsalted nuts, raisins, chocolate and oat-based cereal bars will provide a steady release of energy that will sustain you during endurance pursuits like walking or cycling. Avoid taking any foods that are too salty as they will simply make you thirsty.

▼ *Take high-carbohydrate snacks such as cereal bars or chocolate in your pack to maintain your energy levels during the day.*

**CLOTHING**

Do not overdress. If you set off feeling a little cold, within 15 minutes of starting out you should be feeling just about right. If you set off feeling warm, however, you will be too hot within 15 minutes. If you are in a temperate climate, be prepared for sudden changes in the weather.

Consider the type of terrain you will be travelling through. If you will be walking or cycling through lots of scrub or thick undergrowth, or if there are biting insects in the area, wearing shorts will mean cuts and grazes to your legs and insect bites.

In hot countries you may need to change from shorts to lightweight trousers as the sun's heat increases in order to protect your legs from sunburn. A wide-brimmed sun hat will protect the back of your neck from the sun.

If you are going to be walking over loose rock or sandy soil, some short gaiters over the top of your boots will stop small stones and soil getting into your boots. If the conditions are going to be very wet under foot, you will find knee-length gaiters useful to protect your boots and feet from the mud and water.

If you will be travelling in an area where it is likely to rain, pack your waterproofs at the top of your pack so you can get them out quickly if it starts to rain very suddenly. Items such as maps, guidebooks and a compass can be carried in a large pocket in your clothing or in a plastic document wallet on a cord around your neck. If you have to stop to take them out of your pack each time you need to refer to them, you will slow down the pace or the group and, if you are walking, will find it almost impossible to get into a good rhythm.

**PACKING A DAY SACK**

If you day's route is part of a longer journey you will be carrying your whole pack, but for a one-day outing from an established camp you can carry a smaller pack for the day's needs. These should include some emergency supplies in case of accidents or getting lost:

- Maps, compass and guidebooks
- Small first-aid kit
- Insect repellent and high-factor sun cream and/or sunblock
- Spare socks if walking
- Water
- Trail snacks
- Waterproof clothing
- Extra layer of warm clothing such as a fleece jacket
- A mobile (cell) phone may be appropriate in some situations

# Walking

Most trips will involve some walking, even if the main activity is cycling or horse riding. A short hike is within most people's capabilities, but if you are going to walk 16–19km/10–12 miles or more a day with a pack on your back, daily for several days, your feet and body will suffer if you have not prepared yourself beforehand.

**PREPARATION**

If you are not an experienced walker and are expecting to find your walking trip quite demanding, try to get in some training walks as part of your preparation. Start with gentle walks of 3–5km/2–3 miles a day on easy-going terrain around your home or place of work. Build this up to 16–19km/10–12 miles walking on local footpaths once or twice a week wearing your boots and carrying your pack.

**BUYING NEW BOOTS**

When you go to a store to buy a pair of walking boots, take with you the socks you will be wearing on the trip. Always try the boots on before you buy. Make sure you have plenty of room to move your toes, but not so much room that your foot slips, which can cause rubbing and blisters. If you are unsure about what you need, ask a trained sales assistant to recommend the best boot for you and the conditions you are going to.

New boots need breaking in before you wear them for long walks, so that the inside of the boot is moulded to the shape of your foot. This is particularly important for leather boots. Lightweight fabric boots need less breaking in than leather ones, but you should still wear them around the house for a few days, for half an hour at a time, before going outdoors in them. Even then, wear them on short walks at first, gradually building up the distance.

Think about your overall physical fitness if you are overweight or out of condition, or if you have been ill or are recovering from an injury. On a backpacking trip, where you will be carrying all of your camping and cooking gear, including food and water, you will be carrying considerable extra weight on your feet and legs and putting a greater strain on your body, and you need to be sure that this won't cause health problems or severe discomfort, or aggravate existing injuries.

▲ *A good stout pair of leather mountain boots will be needed if you are going high above the snow line.*

**CARE OF YOUR FEET**

Never underestimate the importance of comfortable feet on a walking trip; uncomfortable or sore feet can make your trip truly miserable, so it is worth taking care of them properly.

Harden your feet before a walking trip by rubbing them with surgical spirit (rubbing alcohol) after washing and drying. Concentrate on the ball of the foot, the toes and around the heel.

During the expedition, keep your toenails cut short, so that your boots don't press on them. Keeping your feet clean will make you more comfortable and washing them every day is advisable; not only does it make good hygiene sense, but it is also hugely refreshing to wash your feet when you return to camp at the end of the day. Dry feet well after washing, and check for sores or blisters before pulling on cotton socks and lightweight trainers or flip flops to wear around camp. Dust feet with an anti-fungal foot powder if they are prone to sweating.

### Deciding on footwear

The most important criteria with walking boots is that they fit you properly. Badly fitting boots can cause discomfort and blisters, and this will be enough to ruin your day. Boots should give good ankle support, and this is especially important for mountain walking. Bear in mind that the same boots will not necessarily be suitable for every trip. For extreme conditions, such as snow and ice, jungle or desert, you will need specially designed boots, because the conditions underfoot are so harsh that your feet and lower legs need extra protection.

For a fine-weather walking trip on well-maintained paths and tracks, strong walking shoes might be just as good as walking boots. They may even be better, because they are not quite so enclosed and will allow your feet to "breathe" better, and this will improve your comfort in hot weather.

### Treating blisters

Some people are more prone to blisters than others, but blisters are very likely to develop on a walking trip if your boots have not been adequately broken in, or if they are fastened too tightly, or if your socks have dirt or sand in the weave. Check your feet after your training walks or when breaking in your boots. Look for any red or pink areas where your boots might be starting to rub. If left unchecked, these could form blisters. Cover any sore areas with adhesive plasters or surgical tape before you wear your boots again.

If you get a stone in your boot or you can feel a fold in your sock while walking, stop immediately and remove your boot to take the stone out or straighten your sock before the friction starts to rub up a blister. If your boots continue to hurt as you walk and you think you are getting a blister, stop as soon as you can and treat the blister or the sore area before it gets any worse. If the skin is just beginning to rub, put a small moleskin patch on it. Moleskin patches are made from adhesive felt and are widely available from pharmacies and drugstores. They provide padding to take the pressure off the sore area as you walk.

If a blister has developed but you have to go on walking, you can drain it if you have a scalpel blade in your first-aid kit. Blisters can turn nasty if they become infected, so drain the blister only if you have a clean scalpel. Poke a small hole in the blister to allow the fluid to drain out, then cover with a clean plaster or moleskin patch to prevent dirt from entering the open blister, and refit your boots.

If you do not drain the blister, you should still cover it with a clean dressing. The aim is to protect the fluid-filled blister sac, so build padding with raised sides and a hole in the middle; do not cover the top of the blister as this will put pressure on the fluid-filled sac and may cause it to burst. Use a moleskin patch with a hole in the middle (or cut a small hole in a flat patch) and secure with plasters before refitting your sock and boot.

At camp, wash your feet and change the dressing on the blister. The next morning, make sure that the blister is well padded before you put on your boots and start walking.

▲ *You may be more comfortable with a backpack harness that allows some air to circulate between the sack and your back.*

▼ *A specially prepared blister kit is useful on any walking expedition. Take action as soon as you feel a sore spot.*

▼ *If you have to ford a stream, don't be tempted to take off your shoes or boots; this could cause you to slip or cut your feet.*

## Socks

Whether you wear two pairs of socks or just one thick pair, change them for a clean pair every day, washing the dirty ones as you go if you do not have enough clean pairs for every day. Walking socks should never have mends in them, as these cause friction against the skin and can lead to blisters.

## WEIGHT OF YOUR PACK

How much weight adult men and women can carry comfortably will depend on their personal fitness levels, how many hours they will be carrying the load, and what sort of terrain they will be walking on. As a general rule, try to keep down the weight of your pack to under 11kg/25lb, as more than this is likely to turn a pleasant walk into an endurance march. With modern lightweight equipment and food rations, especially if you are sharing the burden of carrying equipment with others, your pack need not weigh more than this. If you are walking in hot weather, the amount of water you take with you will increase the weight of your load, and you may need to look at ways to reduce the overall weight of your camp kit to compensate for this.

# Walking Techniques

Everyone knows how to walk: it's not a skill you need to master from scratch before setting off on a trip, but there are some tips and dodges that can ease your way when walking on rough, steep or slippery ground, helping you to avoid accidents and putting less strain on your feet and joints. Developing an easy, elastic stride means that you expend less energy with each step, enabling you to walk longer distances with greater pleasure.

### WALKING AS A GROUP

If you are walking as a group, especially if some members are inexperienced or young, aim to have one experienced adult walker at the very front of the party and another at the very rear so that stragglers don't get left behind.

If the group has more than ten people, you may consider splitting it into smaller parties, as it is not much fun walking as a long crocodile of people for several hours. It is also easier to keep control of a smaller group, making sure everyone keeps together, takes their rest stops at the same time, and does not wander too far from the footpath or route.

The lead walker, at the front of the group, should set the pace, and this should only ever be the pace of the slowest person in the group, although it should be steady. A particularly slow walker should never be left to walk on their own; other members of the group should take it in turns to walk with them to give encouragement. Some people will naturally walk faster than others, but if those at the front of the group do get some way ahead, they should stop and wait for the others to catch up. The front group should never get so far ahead that they cannot be seen by those at the rear.

This is critically important if not everyone in the group is equipped with a map and compass because those at the back may not be sure of the route to follow. The leader can also act as scout, watching out for obstacles or potential hazards and finding the best route across or around them.

▲ *If the group gets split up when walking in remote locations, wearing bright clothing makes people easier to spot.*

▼ *In hostile country, keep your party close together and keep checking the route ahead to warn everyone of upcoming hazards.*

While the group should be careful that the slowest walkers are not left behind, the latter need to do their best to maintain a steady pace. If they dawdle and linger, or demand too many stops, the whole group can become discouraged and impatient and the walk will not be a success.

### WALKING EFFECTIVELY

There is one important way of making your walking more effective, less tiring and safer, and that is to take long strides. If you walk from the hips, rather than from the knees, your strides may be slower but they will be longer, and you will be able to put your feet down carefully and surely.

Each step you take uses up energy, so if you can cover 90cm/3ft with each stride instead of 60cm/2ft, you will be

▲ *When walking up or down steep slopes, particularly on unstable ground, plant each step sideways to the slope.*

▲ *When walking in extreme conditions the party should keep close together, if necessary using a system of ropes.*

covering a lot more ground for the same energy output. It's a good idea to practise lengthening your stride during everyday walking so that it becomes natural to you.

**WALKING UP AND DOWNHILL**

When going uphill, take shorter steps than usual, and keep your body weight forwards, but try to keep to the same walking rhythm that you had on level ground. When walking downhill, again take short steps, keep your body weight back and bend your knees slightly, so that the shock of your downward motion is absorbed by your thigh muscles rather than your knees. Descending can be hard on the knees, especially if you are carrying a heavy pack, and you may want to take more stops to make it easier on your legs. Steep ascents and descents will be much easier if you walk in a zigzag.

**DIFFICULT TERRAIN**

If a slope is composed of sand, snow or loose material, such as scree, stand sideways to the slope and step sideways up or down it. Treat descents over wet grass, rocks or loose ground with care, as even walking boots with good grips can slip. Avoid walking over loose, large rocks and boulders, which may become dislodged and start to fall. Walking poles will help you to keep your balance over uneven ground.

If walking over level snow, you may find the going easier with skis. In an open area, a group should walk in single file and within touching distance of each other, so that if there is a sudden blizzard that cuts visibility, you will know where everyone is. In a very heavy blizzard it is usually safer to stop and take shelter, but if you must keep walking, everyone should walk with one arm on the shoulder of the person in front of them.

**THINK AHEAD AND LOOK AHEAD**

Even if you are following a footpath, look at the features of the landscape around you, such as lakes, rivers or woodland, and check that it matches the landscape shown on your map to ensure you are following the correct route and are walking in the right direction. If you are at all unsure, take a compass bearing.

Always be on the lookout for the easiest route around possible hazards, such as boggy land, streams or unstable rocks, that some in the group may have difficulty with. If walking uphill, be prepared to descend a little if you have to in order to find a safer route upwards, and vice versa. If you cannot see the whole course of a stream or river, do not use it as a route down a mountain, as water will take the shortest route, and this may be over a cliff. Likewise, when descending a hill, make sure you can see the whole slope, as some slopes end in cliffs.

**COUNTRYSIDE ETIQUETTE**

Respect the environment and other users of the countryside when walking, especially in a group.

- Give way to other walkers, cyclists and horse riders.
- Take all litter home with you.
- If you are walking over farmland where crops are growing or livestock are grazing, keep to footpaths, close gates behind you and do not touch or deliberately frighten the animals; if you are walking with a dog, put it on a lead (leash) and do not allow it to approach or worry livestock.
- If you have to walk on roads or tracks that have vehicles on them, walk facing the oncoming traffic, unless you are approaching a sharp bend when it is better to walk on the outside of the corner where you will be seen more easily by the oncoming traffic. Take special care if you come to a blind summit.

# Daily Walking Routine

On a long-distance walk it may take you a few days to settle into a daily pattern of walking, striking a happy medium between feeling relaxed and enjoying a sense of achievement.

**WALKING PROGRAMME**

At what time you start and finish your walk is something for the group to decide between them according to personal preference, but it will also depend on where you are walking and at what time of year.

If you are walking in a temperate or arctic climate in the winter months, there will be fewer hours of daylight than in the late spring, summer or early autumn, and as you will not be able to walk for as long, you will not be able to cover as much distance. You may prefer to walk right through all the few hours of daylight there are before making camp, rather than stopping for lengthy rest stops mid-route.

If you are walking in a hot climate, you may wish to start your walk at dawn and finish in the late morning, around 11am, when the sun will already be very hot. You can either make camp then or rest up in the shade until the mid afternoon, around 3.30pm, when the day will start to cool down and you can move on again.

Try to divide up your day so that your lunch break comes roughly half way through the walk. This is for practical and psychological reasons: it makes sense to restock your energy levels with food and rest halfway through the day, and it makes the day's programme more balanced, so that you are not faced with an unpleasantly long afternoon walk after a short, easy stretch in the morning. You may want to make an exception if you prefer to have lunch at a particular site, such as somewhere with a view or shelter, or where you can replenish your store of water.

**WALKING ALONE**

As a lone walker you will be able to fix your own routine and suit yourself how far you go and when you stop. However, it's still important to take regular rests and not try to walk too far in one day, as the result will be that you won't feel like walking at all the next day.

Provided you have confidence in your navigational skills, you will be free to change your plans and make detours at will. Without the distraction of fellow walkers you will be far more alert to your surroundings and the slow pace will give you time to observe all that is of interest in the landscape.

▼ *Get into a comfortable rhythm, but try to match your companion's pace to avoid the walk feeling like a forced march.*

**REST STOPS**

Try to keep these brief: a 5–10 minute stop every hour on the hour should be enough for most walkers, but be flexible if someone is having a bad day and needs to stop more often or for longer. In hot weather or if the walking is very strenuous and you are sweating a lot, take more stops to have a drink to avoid becoming dehydrated. If you are walking with children, you may need to build in more stops than this, depending on the age and strength of the children, but plan the stops before you set off and be firm with the children if they try to manipulate you to make more stops along the way: the more stops you make, the more difficult it is to get into a good walking rhythm. Likewise, it is a good idea to agree within the group that going to the toilet, drinking and checking the map will all take place during these hourly stops. If you need to drink as you walk, use one of the drinking systems in which you carry the water bag in your pack and drink from a tube leading from it.

When you stop for a long period, such as at lunchtime, or while waiting for slower walkers to catch up, put on an extra layer of clothing to make sure you do not get too cold. If you take your boots and socks off while you rest, be careful not to get your feet too cold or even sunburned, and do not walk around bare-footed in case of thorns or sharp rocks.

When starting your walk after a stop, check the area in case a camp fire has not been put out properly, or items of kit or litter have been left behind.

▲ *Rocky terrain can be hard on the feet and especially on the knees. Be sure to take plenty of brief rests.*

▼ *From a high viewpoint on a good day you may be able to see many miles of the route ahead of you.*

**TAKE EXTRA CARE WHEN TIRED**

Be aware that at the end of the day's walk, when you will be feeling physically tired, your concentration can wander, and it is at this point that accidents are most likely to happen. Don't take short cuts from your route and avoid skipping rest stops in order to get to the campsite quicker: remember that the original schedule was carefully thought through in the first place, and if a rest stop was planned, it is probably needed.

**SICK OR INJURED WALKERS**

If someone in the group becomes injured or unwell on the walk, give them first aid attention straight away. Dress the injury or make them as comfortable as possible. If the casualty is unable to move, the group needs to work out how to fetch help. If the casualty can walk, they should be escorted by a fit person in the group, with the two walking in the middle of the group so as not to be left behind. You may well need to change your route to find the swiftest or easiest way back to camp or to find medical assistance.

# Cycling

Cycle camping trips were traditionally confined to the road system until the arrival of the mountain bike opened up new possibilities of off-road routes not previously available to the cyclist.

## CHOOSING A BIKE

A multi-speed touring bike is comfortable and speedy for road riding, but if you are planning to include rough tracks in your route a mountain bike is more rugged and reliable. Its fatter tyres and heavier frame make it harder work on tarmac and when climbing hills. Hybrid bikes, a compromise between the tough mountain bike and the fast, light tourer, are a versatile alternative.

If you are choosing a new bike, make sure its frame is the right size for you and check that the saddle is comfortable, as a bad saddle will ruin your trip. Buy the best tyres you can afford. The rear tyre will wear faster than the front one, so it can be a good idea to switch them around when they are partly worn.

Before any long trip your cycle should have a full service: if you can't do the servicing yourself take the bike to a specialized cycling shop.

## SETTING UP YOUR BIKE

It's important to ensure that your bike is set up correctly to suit you. This means adjusting the position of the saddle and the handlebars for comfort and maximum pedalling efficiency. With the ball of your foot on the pedal when it is at the bottom of its rotation you should have a slight bend in your leg. When you start pedalling, you should be able to reach the pedals without having to move your hips. If this is not the case you will need to change the height of the saddle.

You'll find that you can adjust your saddle backwards and forwards slightly, as well as tilting it up and down – experiment with this to see what feels most comfortable.

Handlebar height and reach is also a vital consideration. You don't want to be too stretched out as this puts strain on the hands, wrists, arms, shoulders and back, so again experiment with adjusting the bars to find the optimum riding position. If you're not sure how to do this your local bike shop will be able to help. If you are riding a mountain bike you may find that the straight handlebars offer too little variation in hand positions, so that your arms get tired and stiff. Drop handlebars on a touring bike avoid this problem, and you can buy extensions for mountain bike handlebars to give you an alternative grip.

## CLOTHING AND EQUIPMENT

If you are planning a touring trip using a bike as transport, consider your clothing and equipment carefully. You need to keep the weight and bulk down, otherwise you may find the bike becomes too difficult to control. How much you can carry comfortably will depend on your bike and your level of physical fitness, but as a rule, aim to keep the combined weight of your gear below 11kg/25lb: about the same as a walker's backpack.

▼ *Cycling helmets are made of shock-absorbing foam that does not recover: replace any helmet that has suffered an impact.*

### A WELL-FITTING HELMET

A good cycling helmet is a vital accessory, and modern helmets are so lightweight and aerodynamic you'll scarcely notice you're wearing one. Your helmet should fit snugly on your head when fastened, and not be able to move around or slide forward and obstruct your vision. The chin-strap shouldn't be too tight.

▲ *Padded cycling gloves will protect your hands from blisters caused by gripping the handlebars.*

► *Padded cycling shorts act as a cushion to make sitting on a saddle all day more comfortable.*

▲ *A cycling computer can be attached to your handlebars to keep you informed of speed, distance and route gradient.*

▲ *A cyclist's tool kit includes all manner of elements that could come in handy for emergency repairs during your trip.*

▲ *When weight is an issue, a compact multi-tool combining a range of knives, scissors and pliers can be invaluable.*

## Clothing

It is possible to buy specialized bike clothing that will keep you warm (or cool) and dry in virtually any weather conditions. Check guidebooks and local information services to find out what conditions to expect.

Your basic kit should include a helmet, a waist-length waterproof cagoule top and waterproof trousers if you are likely to run into heavy rain. Thermal base layers can be worn beneath your waterproofs. Choose clothing that can be layered and is close-fitting, so it won't flap in the wind or get tangled up with the bike.

Padded gloves will protect your hands from blisters and will also soften the effect of vibration when cycling on rough surfaces. Padded shorts or cycling tights are specially designed for comfort and ease of movement; they are not essential, but are worthwhile if you are planning to cycle long distances. Otherwise, cotton trousers or leggings are appropriate as long as they fit neatly at the lower leg and will not catch on the chain. In warm weather shorts are ideal, but remember to protect your legs with sunscreen.

Some cyclists like to wear clip-in shoes, which attach to the pedals and make for more efficient pedalling, or toe clips; neither of these is strictly necessary. However, you should wear footwear with stiff soles, such as walking shoes: trainers are designed to absorb impact, and will compress with each pedal stroke, wasting your energy.

▼ *This pannier sits at the front of the bike, just below the handlebars. It should be used for items you need ready access to.*

## Luggage

For long journeys it is more comfortable to stow all your luggage on the bike rather than carrying a pack on your back. Use rear panniers strapped to a rigid carrier that keeps the weight evenly distributed over the back wheel. If this is not enough, add front panniers, but make sure they don't interfere with the front wheel or restrict your ability to steer the bike. The general rule when loading luggage is that the weight should be kept as low and as close to the middle of the bike as possible to maintain stability.

Bear in mind that the more kit you carry the harder your ride will be, and with heavily laden panniers your bike will become less manoeuvrable. You should keep items you may need during the day near the top of your panniers for easy access.

## Spares and repair kit

Modern bikes are easy to maintain and relatively cheap to repair and service. If you are going to be away from cycle stores or suppliers for a week or more during your trip, you will need to carry a spare inner tube, a puncture repair kit, a multi-purpose spanner (US wrench), appropriate Allen keys (wrenches), brake blocks and at least one spare brake cable for the back brakes. (The rear brake cable is longer than the front one, so it can be used for either front or back brakes.) It may be worth carrying a spare tyre as well.

If you are travelling as a group, it will be useful if some of your spare equipment can be interchangeable between your bikes, so that you can spread the load. Make sure you have a serviceable pump for your tyres and a small pressure gauge to check the tyre pressures on everyone's bike each morning before setting off.

▼ *Your puncture repair kit should include patches of various sizes, adhesive, abrasive paper and chalk to mark the puncture site.*

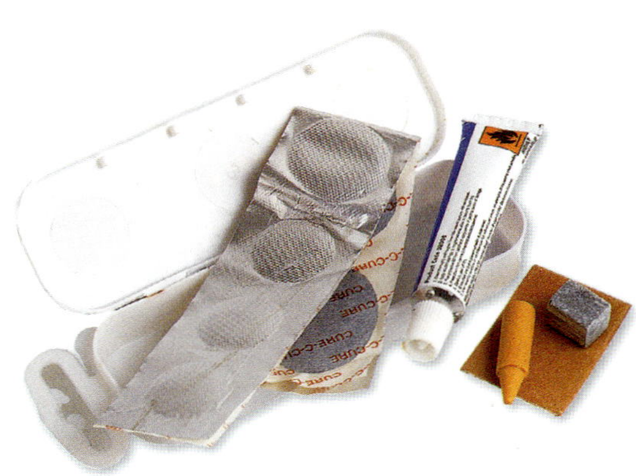

# Cycle Training

Racing cyclists are generally considered to be some of the world's fittest athletes, and cycling certainly does get you fit. Yet you don't have to aim so high to plan an enjoyable trip.

▲ *When going uphill, if the trail is not too steep, riding out of the saddle uses energy less efficiently but produces more power.*

**BUILDING STAMINA**

Whether you are riding on- or off-road you need to build up your training gradually. There is no point in achieving a massive ride on your first day if you are hardly able to get on the bike the next day.

If you are not used to riding a bike, or haven't ridden for some time, you will need time to get your muscles used to propelling a bike and your bottom used to being on a saddle. Regular short rides will build your strength and stamina and you can try a day's ride from home to see how far you can manage comfortably.

As with most sports, the best training for cycling is actually doing it. You can improve your general fitness by doing weights, running or swimming, but by spending more time on your bike you will get fit just as well while at the same time becoming technically more efficient at cycling. Use your gears to get you up the hills – there is no point struggling in one gear if you have an easier one, and remember, you can always get off and walk to rest those leg muscles.

Families can enjoy cycling together both on- and off-road. Because bikes are so simple to use and maintain children find them easy to relate to and enjoy.

▼ *Woodland tracks are bound to be crossed by roots; on descents, slow down before you reach them and rise out of the saddle.*

**RIDING THE BIKE**

Your riding technique will depend on where you ride. All cyclists should obviously be alert to their surroundings, but while a road cyclist's main concern is usually other road users, mountain bikers will find they need to keep a close eye on the rough terrain they're riding over. Always look well ahead and prepare for the rocks and roots you're about to reach rather than looking straight down in front of your wheel – by the time you see objects this close it's too late to take action to avoid them.

The main difference in technique between road cycling and off-roading is one of balance. When cycling down steep off-road sections, get out of the

▲ *Mountain bikes can be safely ridden over small obstacles such as fallen tree branches or sizeable rocks that appear on your path.*

▼ *Familiarize yourself with gear-changing before you set off. Gears will only make pedalling easier if they are used correctly.*

saddle and keep your weight over the back wheel of the bike. If cycling in a group make sure you do not bunch up when going downhill – the results can be disastrous.

Riding single-track paths can also be tricky and potentially hazardous so do practise on some narrow paths in your neighbourhood before planning a long trip off-road. Control is paramount so always stay focused and keep your eyes on the route ahead.

### WORKING OUT A PROGRAMME

Keep your training sessions varied, alternating hard and easy days. Some trails, especially those at mountain bike centres, are graded for difficulty which means you can ensure you don't take on too much when you go out for a ride. Try to find trails that offer a variety of terrain – flat, undulating and hilly, both on- and off-road – as on a long trip you may encounter any of these conditions. When training on hills, vary the length and gradients of the slopes you attempt. Train in wet and windy weather, not just on fine days, so that you are fully prepared for all conditions.

Practise riding at a steady pace over different surfaces and concentrate on developing endurance rather than speed. When travelling you will want to appreciate your surroundings. You need to find a pace that you can maintain comfortably without feeling breathless and exhausting yourself.

### RIDING SAFELY IN A GROUP

The ideal number for your cycling party is four. If anyone has an accident it is safer for two people to go off in search of help, not one, while someone else stays with the casualty. As everyone's abilities and stamina will vary within the group it is important to watch your pace and keep within the capacity of the group as a whole. Do not allow the group to become too strung out and always wait for each other at the bottom of steep hills. Take frequent rests, eat, drink and keep warm to avoid any risk of exposure. Finally, watch out for signs of exhaustion among your fellow riders.

## PUNCTURE REPAIR

**1** Take off the wheel. Make sure you keep all the nuts and bolts safe.

**2** Using tyre levers, ease the tyre off the rim of the wheel.

**3** Carefully remove the inner tube from the tyre, taking care not to damage the valve. Locate and mark the hole.

**4** Gently brush the area around the puncture with abrasive paper to roughen the surface of the rubber.

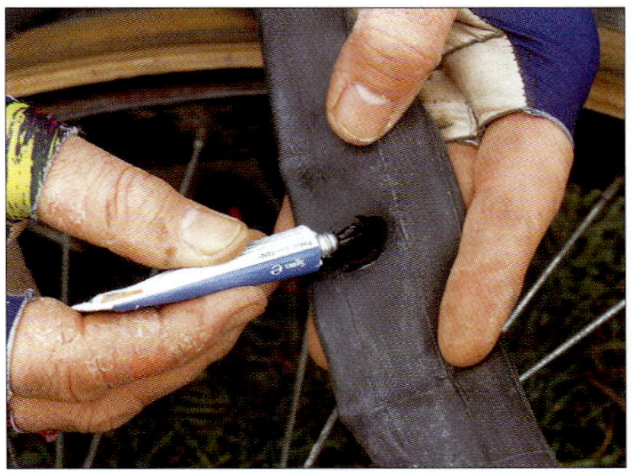

**5** Apply the glue, making sure you cover a large enough area around the puncture to secure the patch.

**6** Put on the repair patch. Hold it down firmly for as long as required by the manufacturer's instructions.

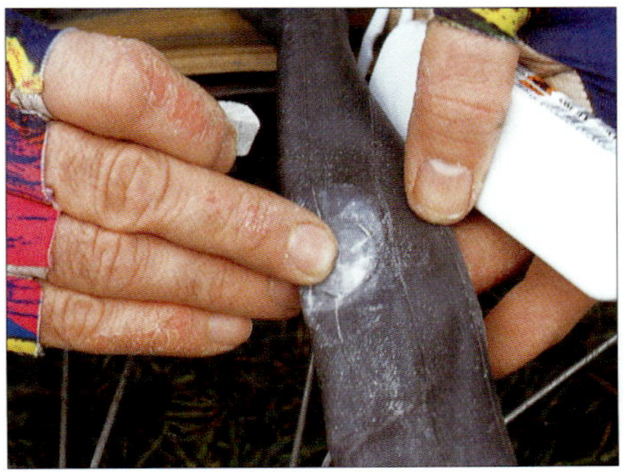

**7** Dust the repair with chalk. Refit one edge of the tyre. Inflate the tube slightly and refit on the rim.

**8** Use your thumbs to tuck the tyre edge back into the wheel rim and inflate the tyre fully.

# Daily Cycling Routine

One of the advantages of travelling by bicycle is its portability. You can easily transport it by plane, boat, train or car, so you can plan your trip anywhere in the world.

### PLANNING YOUR ROUTE

If you are a relative novice, it's wise to choose reasonably flat, well-maintained terrain rather than challenging hills. Beware of absolutely flat countryside, however, as you will have no shelter from the wind and pedalling will be hard if it is against you.

On- or off-road cycling allows you to explore and discover countryside you might never otherwise see. Because you travel so much more slowly than in a car, you have time to take in your surroundings, but because cycling is faster than walking, you can cover more ground. As your fitness develops you'll be amazed at the distances and hills you can tackle.

When planning your day's route, it is worth remembering that you will be able to cover a far greater distance than your walking counterpart. You should reckon on about four times the distance of a walker: about 80–100km/50–62 miles a day. This makes it feasible to plan detours to particular places of interest: an extra 16km/10 miles in a day's cycling may be worthwhile to get the most from the trip, unless the route involves particularly strenuous ascents and descents.

If you are planning to take your bike cross-country, there are now guide books available to show trails and tracks in popular cycling areas. These trails are often graded according to their level of difficulty, and this will be useful if it is an area you are unfamiliar with. Bear in mind that a bike with 9–13kg/20–30lb of extra weight on it will be much less manoeuvrable than an unladen bike.

▼ *In some places drivers may expect cyclists to get out of their way: don't argue with a truck in the middle of the road.*

### MAINTENANCE CHECKS

While on your trip, your daily routine should include checking your cycle at the beginning and end of each day. Use a gauge to make sure that the tyres are inflated to the recommended pressure. Inspecting the treads for embedded stones and other sharp objects may save you the trouble of repairing a puncture later on. Check that the chain and gears are all working and well-oiled. Check the brakes: inspect the brake pads and adjust the tension in the brake cables if necessary. If the cables are too tight the brake pads will be touching the wheel rims; if they're too loose you won't be able to stop.

▲ *When the going gets too rough for the most rugged bike its portability means that you can carry it across obstacles.*

Check the height of the saddle periodically as weight and vibration may lead it to sink slightly over time. If you have marked the correct position on the post it is easy to restore. Check that the lights are working and do not need adjustment.

When you've finished your ride for the day, don't forget to clean and lubricate your bike (this applies especially to mountain bikers). If you leave the mud and grime on it will be harder to shift later, and it can cause damage to mechanisms such as gears and brakes, as well as causing rust to develop. Keeping the chain clean and free of grit will give you a smoother ride and lengthen the life of the chain and cogs. It should be lubricated each time it's cleaned.

**DAY RIDES**

On shorter day rides you won't need anything as big as panniers to carry your gear, but try to find a cycling-specific backpack. It should be big enough to store your repair kit, spare clothes and food and water for the day. Many backpacks are now fitted with a hydration system; they contain a bladder for carrying water with an attached drinking tube so you can drink while on the move. However, they can be difficult to keep clean if you use them for extended journeys.

▲ *Try out the cycle and your own fitness on a number of shorter day trips before you start on a long expedition.*

**LOADING THE CYCLE**

Before setting off in the morning you'll need to stow your camping gear and other luggage on the bike, and doing this neatly and methodically every time is important for your comfort and safety. Make sure that most of the weight is over the back wheel, packed in the rear pannier bags. More gear can be placed on the rear carrier in between the panniers. If you are using front panniers, you must make sure they are packed neatly and will not interfere with the steering of the cycle. Check that all pannier bags are securely attached so they cannot interfere with the wheels once they are turning.

If you are carrying a tent, either strap it on the rear carrier or carry it in one of the rear pannier bags. Spare clothes and cooking equipment should also go at the back. In front will be your stove and food. Light, bulky articles such as your sleeping bag can go on top of the rear panniers.

You may have a pouch on your handlebars for those items that you will need during the day's cycling, such as your waterproofs, your map and compass, and a water bottle. A map board attached to the front of the bike saves time when navigating.

Ensure that all your gear is well secured, cannot interfere with your steering and is well away from the wheels. It is worth considering that most braking systems are designed to stop an unladen bike, so another of your regular safety checks should be to see how they perform when you are fully loaded.

**STOPS AND BREAKS**

If you're cycling in a group, agree on a schedule for regular rest stops, with time for a snack and a chance to consult the map for the next stage. If the group varies widely in fitness and skill, some members may set a considerably faster pace. Agreeing in advance on stopping places will give everyone a chance to catch up. At the end of the day, the fastest cyclists can be persuaded to start setting up camp if they arrive at your destination early.

In hot weather, it may be preferable to have a really early start so that you're riding in the coolest part of the day. You can then take an extended break while the sun is at its hottest. Vary the pace of the trip by building in some easy days and rest days.

▼ *When cycling off-road, be considerate to other users of the countryside and try to minimize your impact on the terrain.*

# Kayak and Canoe Touring

Kayaking and canoeing are very old methods of transportation and can vary from a pleasant paddle along a flatwater river or sheltered coastline to a fast and exciting paddle down a white-water river. The only interruption to a continuous, comfortable journey will be extreme rapids, weirs or non-navigable locks, when the boat will have to be carried overland.

**CHOOSING A BOAT AND PADDLES**

A huge number of kayaks are now available. They are all single-seaters. When choosing a kayak, check that it has sufficient buoyancy to float when full of water; the buoyancy should be distributed so that the kayak floats level when swamped. It must have a seat and a footrest to brace against, otherwise you will not be able to paddle properly.

Canoes are available as single- and double-seaters. A double canoe will accommodate two people, as well as all the supplies necessary for several days of touring. A double canoe can be paddled by one person, but putting two people in a solo canoe is a recipe for a swim. Canoes for three or more people are also available. Double canoes vary from expensive wooden models to cheaper alternatives made of synthetic materials, such as aluminium and polymers, which are more resistant to serious damage if you scrape them over rocks in low-water conditions.

Paddles need to be robust but as light as possible. They also need to be the right length: to check the length of a kayak paddle, stand it up level with your foot, and reach up to grasp the top blade. You should be able to do this comfortably with your arm slightly bent. A canoe paddle is always shorter than a kayak paddle because it has only one blade. Beautifully crafted wooden paddles have the nicest feel, but paddles with alloy shafts and plastic blades are a lot cheaper. If you are buying or hiring a paddle, try out a variety of models before deciding. Always carry a spare set of paddles with you in case of damage or loss.

▼ *A white-water canoe is fitted with airbags to keep it afloat when full of water. These can be removed for paddling flatwater, and the space used to carry your gear.*

▼ *A modern white-water kayak suitable for beginners. This boat could also be used for paddling flatwater and sheltered stretches of coastal water.*

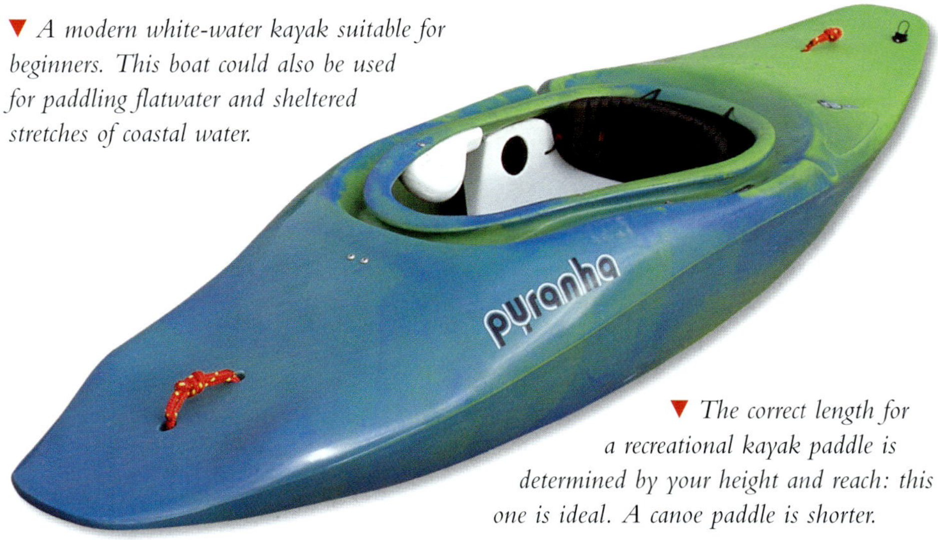


▼ *The correct length for a recreational kayak paddle is determined by your height and reach: this one is ideal. A canoe paddle is shorter.*

**SPRAYDECKS**

A spraydeck (spray skirt) fits around your waist and over the cockpit, and is used with kayaks to prevent water from getting into the boat. It is not generally needed on flatwater, where the water is calm and there is little or no splashing. If you wear a spraydeck, it is essential that you know how to remove it easily, in case you need to exit the boat quickly in a capsize.

▲ *A thermal top worn with board shorts, a buoyancy aid and trainers are ideal clothing for fine-weather paddling.*

**PERSONAL BUOYANCY**

A buoyancy aid (personal flotation device or PFD) is vital to help prevent drowning and should be worn at all times when on the water, no matter how confident a swimmer you are. Choose a style that allows you to move your arms freely, and one that fits snugly and will not pull off when you are in the water. To check the fit, pull firmly upwards from the shoulders: if it can be pulled off, the straps need tightening.

**HEAD PROTECTION**

There is no legal requirement to wear a helmet, but it is advisable to wear one, especially for paddling on white water. Make sure it fits: a helmet that is too big can slip off and one that is too small can cause discomfort. Look for a helmet that carries a recognized safety mark.

**CLOTHING**

Your insulation requirements depend on the weather, so check the forecast before choosing your level of clothing. Whatever you wear should not be too heavy when wet for you to swim in. Polyester and polypropylene are better than cotton for warmth when wet.

If the water temperature is cold and the air chilly or wet, wear a thermal base layer made from polyester fleece or polypropylene, or wear a wetsuit. If wind-chill is an issue, and a wind- and spray-proof cagoule for upper-body warmth. Good features to look for in a cagoule are a waterproof fabric, neoprene cuffs, a comfortable neck seal and an adjustable waist. In fine weather, a T-shirt and shorts can be worn, with something warmer in case you capsize.

**FOOTWEAR**

You cannot paddle well in bulky, heavy footwear, but bare feet are not ideal, as you will need shoes that have a good grip on wet, muddy banks. Light pumps or technical sandals are light enough to swim in if you capsize. Wetsuit boots and water-sports shoes have good grips, and are padded and reinforced in all the right places, but this is specialized footwear and not strictly necessary for one-off paddlers.

▼ *Additional items might include a hand pump, knife, compass, VHF radio, transistor receiver, flares, sunscreen and a mobile phone.*

▼ *Suitable warm-weather footwear includes technical sandals, which are lightweight, comfortable and widely available.*

▲ *A cagoule offers good protection from the rain, but choose a close-fitting, waist-length style that allows full upper-body movement.*

▼ *A correctly fitting helmet sits on the head without sliding forward. A helmet that does not fit will not give adequate protection.*

▼ *Specialist water-sports shoes will keep the feet warm even when wet, and are a good investment if you plan to paddle frequently.*

# Kayak and Canoe Training

Canals and lakes are good training areas when you are acquiring paddling skills, and will often be adjacent to suitable camping land. The one essential requirement before you begin is the ability to swim. You should be able to swim at least 50m/170ft in the clothes you will be wearing in the boat.

## CROSS-TRAINING

Improving your general level of fitness will dramatically increase the fun you get from paddling, and reduce the likelihood of injury and tiredness. While paddling vigorously or over a long distance is itself an excellent all-body workout, extra non-paddling exercises such as swimming, cycling or running will benefit your cardiovascular system and build body strength before your trip. Whatever cross-training you choose, do it in moderation but aim to exercise regularly – daily if possible.

Target specific muscle groups with toning exercises. The muscles in the thighs, abdomen, shoulders and back do most of the work in the boat, and press-ups, pull-ups and crunches are good preparation for paddling.

## WARM-UP ROUTINE

Start with some light exercise, such as brisk walking, swimming or playing with a frisbee, to warm up and raise your heart rate. Gently stretch each muscle group. Once afloat, take a short paddle then do some more stretches in the boat, leaning backwards and forwards and rotating the trunk.

## CAPSIZE DRILL

If you are going to paddle a canoe or kayak you must know what to do if it capsizes. All beginners should learn this as soon as they start out on the water, and most instructors make it a priority.

When a capsize happens you have a surprisingly long time to react. Should you get out of the boat before it goes over, or wait until it has capsized? If you try to get out you run the risk of being hit on the head by the gunwale. It is better to wait until the boat has stopped moving.

Keep hold of your paddle and boat if possible; do not climb on top of the boat. In a real capsize situation, once you are out of the boat you should find your partner, if you have one, and make sure he or she is fine. See if the river is shallow enough for you to be able to stand on the riverbed, but be wary of the current. If possible, get the canoe and yourself to the shore. In the last resort, you may need to undertake a deep-water rescue with the help of the rest of your party.

**SAFETY RULES**

- Never paddle on your own.
- Always wear your buoyancy aid (personal flotation device).
- Warm up before paddling.
- Know where you are going and, if you do not know the river, check for any rapids.
- Cover any cuts or grazes with waterproof plasters before canoeing to avoid infection.
- Always secure the equipment that you are carrying in your boat.
- Always get help to move a canoe when on land.
- Make sure you wash your hands or take a shower after paddling and before eating.

▼ *For novices in search of trouble-free water in which to practise paddling, inland lakes are the best location of all.*

▼ *You should not attempt to paddle on fast-flowing water until you are confident that you have mastered a range of skills.*

▼ *Weirs can be extremely dangerous for paddlers, and it is always advisable to stay away from them.*

## CAPSIZE AND GET OUT

**1** To practise the capsize sequence, start from your usual paddling position, sitting or kneeling upright in the canoe.

**2** Let go of the paddle with one hand and take hold of the gunwale of the boat.

**3** Lean over to one side until the boat overbalances. Keep hold of the paddle as,you go over.

**4** Allow the boat to capsize. Continue to hold on to the paddle with one hand and the gunwale of the boat with the other.

**5** Stay in the boat until you are completely upside down and the boat has stopped moving.

**6** Kick away from the boat and come to the surface – ideally you should still be holding both the boat and the paddle.

## GO TO THE FRONT AND SWIM

**1** Swim to the front of the boat. If at all possible continue to hold on to the boat and the paddle.

**2** Take hold of the front of the canoe, leaving it upside down.

**3** Using the paddle if you can, and propelling yourself with your arms and legs, swim the canoe to the shore or to other paddlers in your group.

# Daily Routine on a Paddling Trip

If you are taking your first canoe or kayak trip on a canal, many waterside campsites provide excellent facilities and local farmers will rarely turn you down if you ask before camping on their land. Beware of animals in rural areas, particularly in spring when they will have their young with them.

The tent you normally use for camping/backpacking will be fine. Always pitch it well above the water level of a river or lake as water can rise quickly. If the weather will be reliably fine, you could use your boat instead, rigging up plastic sheets or a groundsheet to make a shelter.

▲ *A sea kayak has little storage space but offers the possibility of extended sea journeys into remote areas full of wildlife.*

### COOKING AND EATING

Although cooking on open driftwood fires gives a real sense of outdoor living, many places ban it or allow it in only designated areas. It is a good idea, therefore, to take a simple gas stove with a built-in flint, plus a few pans.

Ensure you take high-energy food supplies, as you will need them to power your muscles and generate warmth while paddling. There are plenty of instant savoury meals and desserts now available from outdoor shops in a wide variety of flavours; read the packaging to check on the calorific value.

If your water supply is suspect, boil it on your stove to kill any bacteria.

### KEEPING THINGS DRY

Your main concern when preparing to get afloat each day will be packing your belongings into the boat. All your equipment needs to be kept as dry as possible, which is not always easy in the case of rain or an inadvertent capsize.

Plastic waterproof drums, which come in a variety of shapes and sizes, are ideal for canoes. They are not too large to carry when loaded, and have easily re-sealable waterproof lids. Specialized waterproof bags are also convenient, as they pack slightly more easily in the boat. Buy different colours or ones with see-through sides, so that you do not keep getting out your dry underwear when you want your lunch.

When packing up your tent, make sure the poles and pegs are attached securely, or stow them separately in a special bag so that you do not lose them if you capsize.

Tying all your bags and equipment into the thwarts is always a very sensible decision, since any capsize could lighten your load instantly, and possibly disastrously.

▼ *The inside of a kayak is an enclosed space, which makes it difficult to pack. Kit needs to be divided between several bags.*

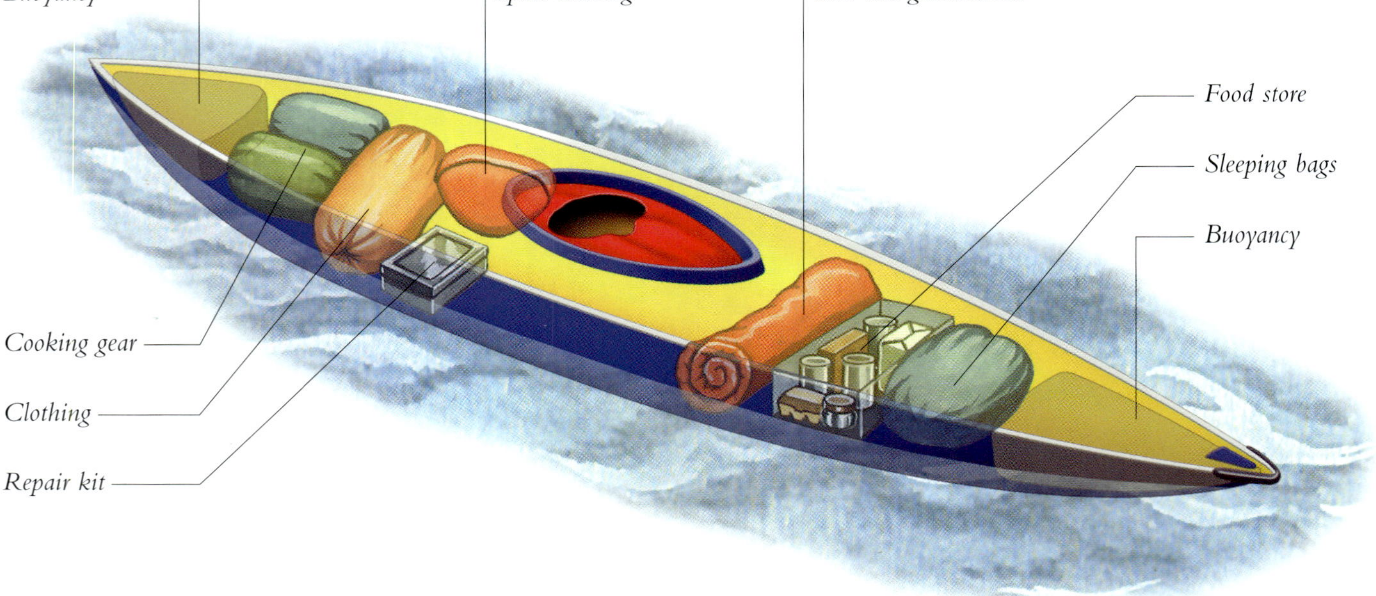

▲ *Durable plastic containers, known as "BDHs", are ideal for storing small items that must be kept dry.*

▶ *Two paddlers carry their loaded sea kayaks down to the water. Hold the boat end grabs, one in each hand.*

**PACKING**

A double canoe can easily accommodate all the supplies and equipment necessary for days of cruising, but in a kayak the space is much more confined. Merely getting all your equipment into the boat can be difficult. Rather than keep your kit in one large bag, the secret is to use several small waterproof bags, known as dry bags, which can be packed more easily into the spaces available. Careful packing is essential.

With a canoe, the balance of the boat will determine how easy it is to paddle, so, taking into account the weight of the paddlers (usually, the heavier paddler sits at the back), try either to weigh or estimate the weight of the different bags, then distribute them evenly in the boat to achieve a level trim.

Pack everything into the boat in the reverse order to which you are likely to need it, and keep your map and compass, water bottle and snacks to hand. Most importantly, never have anything positioned in the boat that would impede your exit or that you could get tangled up in if you need to get out in a hurry.

▶ *Use a roll-top dry bag for essentials such as phones, money and keys.*

▶ *Sea kayaks are equipped with watertight hatches, but you should put your belongings in waterproof bags in case of leaks.*

▶ *More than one boat can be transported on a roof rack, and carrying them vertically reduces wind resistance. Both boats must be placed centrally between the roof bars.*

# Travelling by Horse

Horseback expeditions are a great way for families and non-walkers to visit remote rural areas. You need to think about how you are going to provide food and water for the horse, as well as for yourself, but, in general, this is an enjoyable way to travel, allowing you to ramble across the countryside, taking photographs and absorbing the wilderness scenery all around you.

▲ *A wide-brimmed hat will cut out the glare of intense sunlight, but it offers little head protection in the event of a fall.*

## CHOOSING YOUR HORSE

For a successful expedition on horseback, it is important to have the right horse. If you are hiring a horse from a trekking centre, find out how much experience he has of carrying riders and gear, and as much as you can about his personality. Some countries have their own training systems for trekking horses, so ask about the training your horse has had.

Get to know not only your own horse but also the other horses in your group trip, finding out which horse prefers to follow the others and which is the slowest traveller. Your pace will be dictated by the slowest horse. Find out if the horses you are going to ride are familiar with people who may have little or no riding experience, and if any packhorses you need are used to being loaded with the equipment you intend to use.

Ask about the stabling arrangements you will be expected to provide, and if the horses will be happy to spend the night outdoors in an unfamiliar area.

## CLOTHING

There is little you need in the way of specialized clothing, but when choosing what to wear the keynote is safety.

In many countries, riders wear hard hats, securely fastened with a chin strap, as a matter of course, but this may not be a legal requirement, and you should check if a hat can be borrowed along with the horse, or whether you must take your own. A fall from a horse can be fatal, and a hard hat will always reduce the likelihood of serious injury.

Safe footwear is equally important. Riding boots, jodhpur boots or any leather boot with a smooth sole and a clearly defined heel will prevent the foot from sliding through the stirrup, or becoming caught in the stirrup in the event of a fall, which is a potentially fatal situation. Trainers and boots and shoes with ridged soles and little or no heel should never be worn for riding.

Clothes should be well-fitting and neat without being restrictive. A shirt with a sweater or fleece jacket, and a pair of comfortable trousers, jeans or jodhpurs are ideal. Dark colours will stay smart for longer, and long sleeves are preferable to short sleeves, since they offer some protection from nips from equine teeth. No matter how warm the weather, avoid wearing sleeveless suntops or beachwear.

▼ *The crash hat can be worn with a silk or velvet covering (back left and right); the riding hat (front) is traditional headgear.*

▼ *Short leather jodhpur boots can be worn on their own with riding trousers, or with half-chaps to protect the rider's lower leg.*

▼ *Long riding boots can be made of leather or rubber. The narrow shoe and low heel prevent the foot getting caught in the stirrup.*

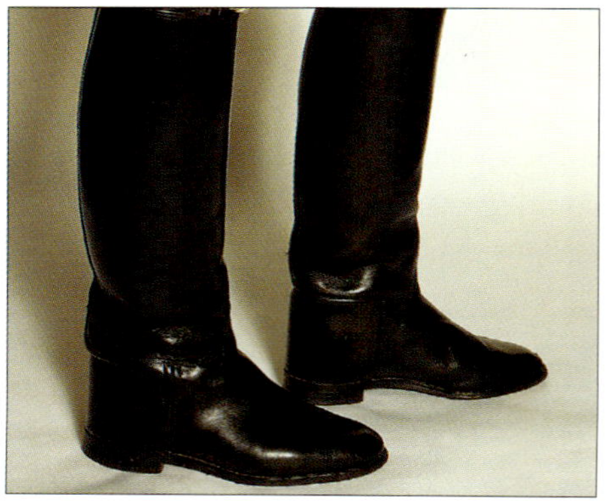

◀ *The essential grooming kit: (clockwise from far left) body brush and metal curry comb, dandy brush, water brush, rubber and plastic curry combs, hoof pick with brush, and cactus cloth.*

▲ *A saddle pannier is fitted to the saddle, positioned behind it, with the pockets hanging over the sides of the horse.*

▼ *A trail pad is a fleece numnah attached to a canvas cloth. The side pockets provide useful easy-access storage for smaller items.*

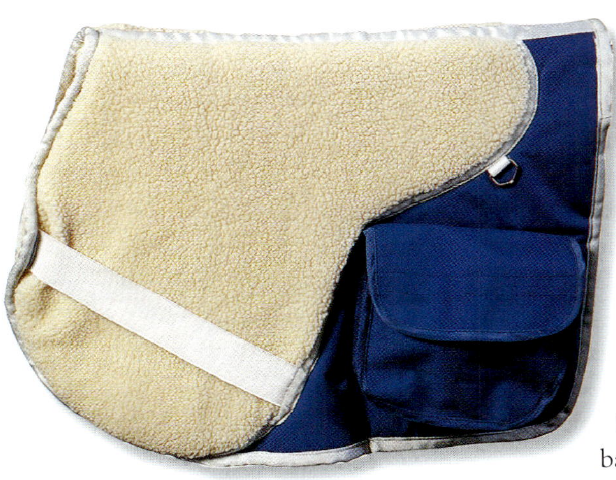

Wear jackets and shirts buttoned up, as a flapping shirt can frighten a horse, and there is the danger that the shirt could become caught on a tree branch if you are riding through woodland. Some horses may be nervous of noisy waterproof fabrics. Long hair should be tied neatly to avoid scaring the horse or becoming caught. Prominent jewellery, such as earrings and bangles, can cause injury if they become caught up.

### EQUIPMENT

Horses are powerful animals and they can carry a considerable weight, but hot weather and long distances are an additional strain, and it is still important to keep your camp kit light, so as not to overload the horse. As well as your own camp kit and clothing, you need to think about the horse's tack, a basic grooming kit, and, depending on how much grass you expect along the route, enough feed for the trip. If you will be in a remote area, carry a spare set of reins and spare stirrup leathers in case your first set become damaged.

### PACKING THE HORSE

Panniers designed for horses are available, and these can be fixed over the back of the saddle. Make sure that no item of kit is sticking into the horse's back or side, and avoid having any equipment hanging off the saddle or pannier, as this could spook the horse. All of your gear should be packed into bags or rolls, and the weight of the load should be balanced on the horse.

### PICKING OUT HOOVES

Picking up one foot at a time, use the hoof pick to scrape dirt and stones from the underneath of the hoof, working from the horse's heel towards the toe. After removing large pieces of debris, use the brush on the hoof pick to clean remnants of dirt from the triangular part of the hoof at the heel, known as the frog. The frog is sensitive and easily damaged, so work gently.

### FITNESS AND TRAINING

A horseback trek is a far gentler way to visit the open country than walking or cycling, and physical fitness is not a priority. Also, you do not need to be an experienced equestrian as the horses are likely to be mild and steady and you will rarely break out of a trot. However, anyone who has never ridden is advised to spend some time on horseback before they go to make sure they feel comfortable in the saddle.

▼ *If you are an inexperienced rider, taking a course of lessons before the trip will give you the confidence to perform the basic commands.*

# Daily Routine on Horseback

Taking care of the horses' needs is one of the main tasks on a mounted trek. The agenda for every day has to be planned with the horses in mind.

▲ *Horseback treks are a hugely enjoyable way to travel across open country, but good planning and preparation are essential.*

**ON YOUR ROUTE**

Spend some time working out your route before you travel, and ask advice from local people or riding institutions as to which trails will be suitable for horses, including where water will be available for the horses to drink. Try to keep to trails constructed with horses in mind, if possible. If you will be following a popular route, plan to take rest stops or breaks for lunch at areas where you will be able to tether the horses off the trail, so that they are not blocking the route for other users.

The etiquette of wilderness trails is that walkers, vehicles and cyclists all give way to horses. Not everyone you meet will be prepared to do this, however, so be on your guard when riding past other trail users, because sudden movements or noises, such as the revving of a car engine, can spook your horses. If you meet another horse party, then those coming downhill should give way to those going up.

**SAFETY CHECKLIST**

- Wear your own properly fitted hat, with the chin strap fastened, at all times when mounted.
- After a fall, replace a hat that has been subjected to impact.
- Wear safe footwear at all times when mounted and use the correct stirrup iron size – about 2.5cm/1in wider than your boot.
- Avoid riding on roads if visibility is poor or at night.
- Do not wear jewellery.
- Ride with your coat fastened, and don't take off a coat or sweater while mounted.
- If your eyesight is not perfect, wear soft contact lenses if possible. If not, ask your optician about the safest spectacles.

**CAMP ROUTINE**

Try to select a well-drained, level stretch of land, and picket the horses at least 60m/200ft away from each other and well away from any water, such as a lake or river, which they could contaminate with urine or droppings. Aim to make camp when there are at least two hours of daylight left, so that the horses have time to graze before it gets completely dark.

However tired you may be, you must deal with your horse before you tend to your own needs. Remove the saddle and bridle, and fit the headcollar, then groom him and provide him with food and water. Visually check the horse's head, body and hooves and run your hand over the back where the saddle has been, and down all four legs. Treat any sore spots immediately, using equipment from your equine first-aid kit. Clean out the hooves with a hoof pick, and brush off any mud from the legs and body, using a body brush.

The next morning, before refitting the saddle and saddle pannier or trail pad when tacking up the horse, check that there are no burrs or small sticks attached to the saddle area of the horse, which could cause sore spots on his back during the course of the day.

**FEEDING HORSES**

Unless you have had confirmation that grass or feed will be available for the horses at your camping ground, do not assume that it will be. Buy an adequate supply of appropriate horse feed from the organization that supplied the horses, or else provide your own.

If you decide to take horse feed with you abroad, check to see if there are rules and regulations about the kind of feed you can take into the country. You may need a certificate stating that

▲ *Your horse is your responsibility for the duration of the trek. If you make friends with him, he is more likely to cooperate.*

the feed is free of weed seed, as proof that there is no danger of contaminating the area with potentially poisonous or non-native weeds.

The horses will need to eat a good meal once a day. It doesn't matter what time they eat, but for convenience, it makes sense to feed them in the early evening, as soon as you have made camp, and before you prepare your own meal. Try to feed the horses at roughly the same time every day and make sure there is enough water for them to drink. Horses do not need to drink purified water, but their water supply should be as clean as possible, free from chemical pollutants, rotting vegetation and litter.

**WILD ANIMALS**

If wild animals, such as bears, wolves, hyenas or big cats could be a danger to you or your horses, ask for a safety briefing before you set off from the organization you hire the horses from, and carry required safety equipment, such as a rifle, with you. If it is a high-risk area, remember that food smells can attract animals from a great distance. Pack away unused food and burn food waste. Rather than leaving the horses free or hobbled to graze at a distance from camp, it is safer to keep them in camp, tied to a stock line.

▲ *Choose a campsite where there will be space to tether the horses. If it doesn't have grazing land, you will need to carry feed.*

▼ *Discipline is needed for horses and riders when travelling on horseback in large groups.*

# Travelling with Pack Animals

If you are venturing into areas inaccessible to vehicles you must either restrict your baggage to the amount you can carry in a backpack or employ one or more pack animals to carry your load for you.

## MULES AND DONKEYS

In areas of the world where the terrain is rocky and steep, the animals of choice for transporting people and heavy loads are mules or donkeys. Both have the ability to survive in conditions where horses and camels do not.

Mules have been used as transport animals for many centuries, though they have a tendency to be bad-tempered and stubborn, and may kick or bite if provoked. They therefore need firmer handling than donkeys. They are the stronger animal, and are capable of carrying up to 100kg/220lb if expertly loaded. They can travel at a good speed but have very wide backs, so riding them for long periods can cause discomfort. Donkeys are smaller and slower, carrying up to 50kg/110lb and requiring to be led on foot. They are gentler than mules, and are very sure-footed in mountain areas.

▲ *Mules are proverbially stubborn animals but will usually respond well if they are treated with kindness.*

### Animal handlers

It will usually be advisable to employ handlers to take care of any pack animals you are using. Unless you have experience of pack animals, dealing with them on your own can be difficult and time-consuming. The handlers will be familiar with the animals, and will know how much weight they can carry, what they need to eat and drink, and how long they need to rest; the animals are likely to respond better to the handlers than they will to you.

This frees you up from taking responsibility for the animals and gives you more time to enjoy the trip. You will be grateful for this if the route is demanding and the living conditions

▼ *Donkeys are better suited to carrying gear than people, and travel at a pace slow enough to appreciate the wilderness.*

▼ *In this sort of rocky country it is better to hire mules or donkeys for use as pack animals rather than camels.*

difficult, but travelling with animal handlers does need to be thought through. If no one in your group can speak the handlers' language, you will need to employ someone who can speak to them on your behalf.

It will need to be agreed whether your team is responsible for providing food and water for the animals and their handlers while they are with you. If you are providing it, allocate it as needed, so that it doesn't all get consumed at the beginning. This is especially true of drinking water. If you are carrying the water you need for your entire trip, issue just the required amount each day (as you would to other team members) or you may find that water gets wasted and you could run out.

### Checking equipment

If you are riding a mule, check the equipment that the animal will have on its back. Is the saddle comfortable to sit in? Are the stirrups in good condition? Are the pack frames suitable for the equipment you wish to carry?

### Hiring agreement

Negotiate an agreement for use of the animals before you set off on the route. The agreement should include the costs to hire the animals, the services of their handlers, food costs for the animals and the handlers, plus any additional equipment you may have to provide or pay for, such as tents for the handlers and equipment for the animals.

Try to make the hire agreement with a reputable tourist organization, or in the presence of a respected local, such as the local chief, a priest at a mission station or the officer commanding the local police, to give you some back-up if there turns out to be a misunderstanding about what was agreed. It may also be wise to pay the handlers in their company, though pay only half upfront, keeping the second half back until you are safely back at base. If you have doubts about the trustworthiness of the animal handlers or owners, you may find that offering an additional sum if all goes well will help to make your trip go smoothly.

#### ANIMAL HANDLING

If you travel without a handler, you will have to take responsibility for a pack animal yourself:

- Feeding and watering: once unloaded, the animal can either be let loose to graze, hobbled or picketed for the night.
- Grooming: caked mud and dust should be brushed out before loading. Hoofs need checking.
- Loading: Make sure the saddle is straight and the load equally weighted on both sides.
- Leading: it may take a few days to get animals going at a steady pace.

▲ *Dog power enables you to visit the most remote wilderness areas, and sledding is an increasingly popular form of adventure travel.*

### DOGS

Sled dogs have been working for centuries in Arctic and subarctic regions. In Alaska they were much used during the 1896 Gold Rush, proving far more hardy and reliable than ponies.

The dogs are bred to haul loads and work in teams, and are very sociable, strong and hardy. They have the highest metabolic rate of any mammal and require a large amount of fresh meat every day. Alaskan Malamutes are long-legged and ideal for pulling loads in deep, soft snow; Siberian Huskies are smaller but faster.

A team of seven dogs can travel about 32km/20 miles a day pulling a sled with a load of about 270kg/600lb – known as a "rig". The teams are carefully assembled: three leading dogs, usually female, are chosen for their intelligence; the middle pair are the speed-dogs and regulate the pace of the whole team; the two nearest the sled are known as the wheel-dogs – normally male, they provide the pulling power.

You can hire teams of dogs and sleds together with experienced handlers, or "mushers" (an Inuit term meaning "one who travels through snow on foot"). This gives you the option of travelling on skis alongside the teams, but the mushers can also offer training in sledding and dog handling. The dogs respond to shouted commands, such as "haw" to go left and "gee" to go right. The key to successful sledding is to relax and loosen up so that you take bumps and twists in the trail in your stride, rather than being thrown off.

# Travelling by Camel

Camels are ideal pack animals for the desert as they can go for long periods without needing food or water. However, camels are temperamental animals: they can bite and kick, and they get upset by strange people, so it is important to keep your distance and to carefully follow any instructions given by their handlers.

**PLANNING YOUR TRIP**

The camels will set the pace of your journey at around 6.5km/4 miles per hour. You will need to establish contact with guides and camel owners at your departure point, which is best done through personal recommendation. Once you have found a local guide you believe to be reliable, it is wise to let him choose the camels for you.

**HANDLING CAMELS**

When you first meet your camel, keep your distance and do not pet it, or you risk getting bitten or kicked. On the first morning, let the handlers do the loading, but assist by carrying loads over to them. If you want to help, ask the handlers what you should do.

Once you get more used to your camel and lose your fear of it, and vice versa, you can become more involved in handling it. Be firm and gentle, and if it tries to misbehave, stand your ground and correct its behaviour.

**LOADING CAMELS**

Your belongings are likely to deteriorate very quickly as they will be exposed in desert conditions and it is always possible that a camel will fall, roll over or shed its load. It is best to pack everything in hardwearing but pliable canvas bags that will not dig into the animal's skin. If you need to carry boxes containing such things as photographic equipment, make sure they are securely roped on top of the load with enough padding beneath to avoid injury to the camel. Water can be carried in skin containers that can be roped on either side of the camel. Make sure you have plenty of rope.

▲ *Use a muzzle if you do not want a camel to eat or if it is causing problems by trying to bite.*

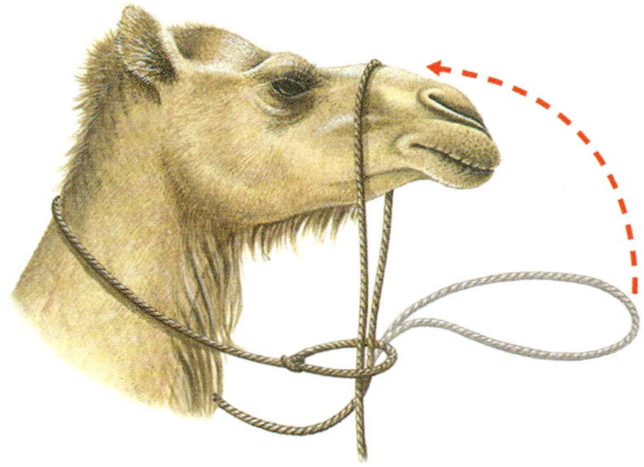

▲ *To fit the head rope, pass the end round the neck then bring a length of the rope through the loop and over the nose.*

▼ *The camel must kneel down to have the saddle fitted. If it tries to rise, hobble the front legs to prevent it.*

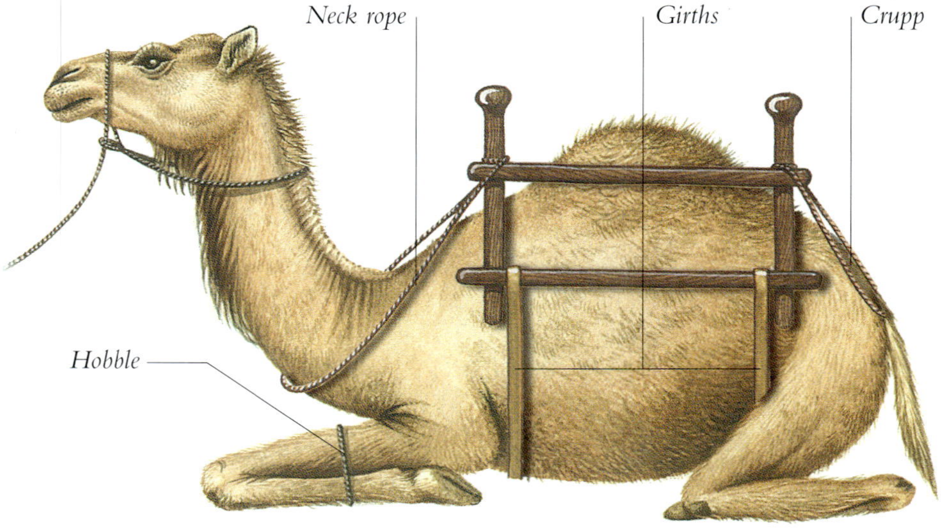


▼ *View of the saddle from the front. The padding must fit snugly to the shoulders and the saddle should not touch the spine.*

▼ *View of the saddle from the rear. The saddle should be at the front and completely clear of the camel's behind.*

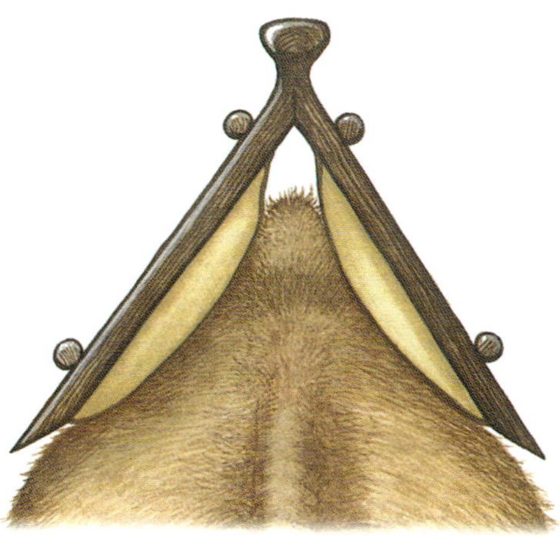

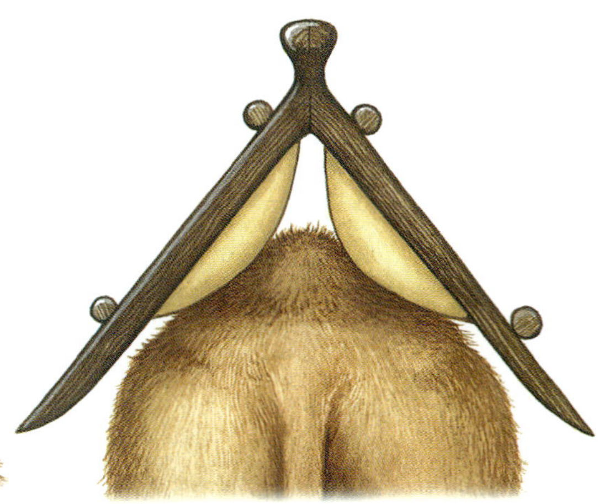

**WHAT TO TAKE**

- Comfortable boots. Though hot, they will protect your feet from sun and thorns. When riding a camel you will need to take them off to avoid chafing its neck.
- Loose-fitting cotton clothes and headgear for protection against sun and insects.
- Warm clothing: the night-time is very cold in the desert.
- A warm down sleeping bag and groundsheet. The sleeping bag can be used as extra padding on the saddle when riding.
- Sunglasses to protect against glare.
- Sunscreen or sunblock.

▲ *Camels like to proceed in order: some animals like to be in front while others will prefer to follow.*

Try not to make any sudden movements or sounds around the animal when loading, and always be alert to what the camel is doing: they do not like being loaded so may attempt to bite or kick.

Fit the head rope first, then couch the camel (make it kneel down) to the command of "too". If it tries to rise, hobble it before fitting the saddle. The load must be of equal weight on both sides and tied up as high as possible.

**DURING THE TREK**

Camel treks usually take place in hot and dry desert climates. Because of this, the trek will start at first light so that the day's distance can be covered before the heat is at its most intense: at midday until the early afternoon. Aim to trek for the first two hours without breaks in order to cover as much ground as possible while the temperatures are relatively low; as it gets hotter, you can stop for five minutes every hour.

The animals should be checked every now and then to make sure that the saddles and their loads are not loose or slipping, otherwise the camels may develop sores on their backs and/or you may lose your kit.

There should always be a handler at the front to lead the train and one at the rear to watch out for any kit that falls off a camel's load. Always keep within eyesight of your camels and handlers, as they know the route and it is very easy to get lost in bush country.

**MAKING AND BREAKING CAMP**

Camp should be made around lunchtime to avoid walking in the heat of the day and to give the camels the six hours they need for browsing before they are brought in for the night. Ideally, choose somewhere upwind of where the camels will be spending the night, as they do smell. Check all the camels each evening with your head handler to make sure they are properly hobbled and to check for sores or tender spots. These must be treated before you start your trek the next day.

▼ *Camels are able to eat and live off almost any kind of scrub, but need several hours of grazing each evening.*

# Vehicle Transport

If you are going to use one or more vehicles on your expedition, you have to decide what type you will need and whether you are going to ship your own out to the expedition area or hire what you need there.

For off-road expeditions in remote areas you should take at least two vehicles, ideally three, so that if one breaks down it can be towed to safety. You will need four-wheel drive if you are intending to drive in boggy or sandy conditions. At the expedition area you will need to pay attention to loading and maintenance. You should be confident that you can service the vehicle yourself, and if necessary attend a vehicle maintenance course before setting off.

▲ *Travelling by motorcycle can be exhilarating, but care must be taken not to destabilize the bike by overloading.*

**TAKING YOUR OWN VEHICLE**

The downside of taking your own vehicle out to the expedition area is that you will be faced with all the costs and bureaucracy involved in this process. The upside is that you will have a vehicle that you know will be in good working order, with all the necessary spares and tools, and which you are confident of driving.

**HIRING A VEHICLE**

If you are hiring a vehicle from a local company, look it over first to check all the tyres, suspension, steering, lights and brakes, and ask to take it on a test drive. Choose your vehicle carefully: a long wheelbase will give you more space but will lack manoeuvrability; the most powerful vehicles will cope with any terrain but will use a lot of fuel. Petrol engines are lighter and more powerful than diesel, but the latter cope well in very low gear so are more reliable in rough terrain. They use less fuel, and diesel fuel is often very much cheaper than petrol.

In some countries you must have a driver, whereas in others you will have the choice of driving the vehicle yourself. The advantages of having a local driver are that he will know the country, will be used to driving on its roads and can be your interpreter. The disadvantages are that you lose a seat in the vehicle, you may not get on with the driver, or even understand him, and he may not be prepared to follow your route. Make sure you can work together before you hire him and the vehicle, and promise a good tip if the trip goes well.

**SPARES AND MAINTENANCE**

Check that you have a spare wheel with a good tyre on it that is inflated, a jack and a tyre spanner (wrench). Also make sure that the hirer has provided any other items that are required, such as a fire extinguisher,

◀ *When hiring vehicles make sure you have thought through the conditions you will be driving in so that your transport is suitable.*

first-aid kit and warning triangle. If you are going to be off-road for any time, you should also have spare oil, inner tubes for the tyres and a puncture repair kit including tyre levers, along with a full set of tools.

Always keep your fuel tank as full as you can, and never pass up the chance of buying fuel. If it is not clean, use a large funnel with a filter in it to filter the fuel before putting it into the tank.

Each night when you have finished your driving for the day, inspect the whole vehicle, especially the tyres, oil level, radiator fluid level and so on.

**LOADING**

How you load the vehicle is important, and if you are going off sealed roads you should keep your loading down to about three-quarters of the manufacturer's recommended limit.

**DRIVING AT NIGHT**

Be wary of driving at night in developing countries, as many vehicles have faulty lights and vehicles may be parked or abandoned without any warning lights or signs.

**DRIVING IN DIFFICULT TERRAIN**

Err on the side of caution: drive slowly and if necessary stop and check the state of the road or track ahead on foot. Stay in the middle of muddy tracks, taking care not to spin the wheels or ground the engine on rocks. Use four-wheel drive except when on firm road surfaces. If you do get bogged down in mud or sand, try reversing out or get your passengers to push. Failing this, dig in front of the wheels to create a gradual slope and try to go gently forwards. Lay down wood, canvas or anything that will help the wheels grip.

**MOTORCYCLES**

In temperate regions a motorcycle can be an attractive option if you are travelling alone. A heavy-duty bike will be able to cope with almost any terrain but will need constant servicing: wash it daily and check all the connections.

The amount of luggage you can take will be strictly limited, and will need to include spare parts and tools. Keep the heaviest weight above the rear wheel and don't load too much on the back as it could destabilize the front wheel. Side panniers should be as slim as possible to reduce wind resistance.

If you are travelling in areas where motorcycles are unfamiliar, take extra care around other road users.

▲ *Snow chains should be fitted either on all four wheels or on the rear wheels only. Make sure the tyres are at the right pressure otherwise the chains will damage them.*

▼ *Getting your vehicle out of heavy mud is a skilled job and should be practised before you embark on a trip.*

# Index

ACKNOWLEDGEMENTS

The publishers would like to thank the following for their valuable contributions to this book:
**Text contributors**
Nick Banks for extra navigation text; Colin Drake for help with the section on physical fitness; Bill Mattos for kayaking and canoeing text; Will Patterson for additional cycling text.
**Text advisors** Peter Tipling, Dr Bill Turner, J. Evans, Mrs A. Funnel.
**Advice and assistance** Malcolm Creasey, Sue Dowson, Andy Middleton, David Williams.
**Models for photography** Doncaster Scout Group, Joe O'Brian, Robert Driskel, Mr and Mrs Gibson, Lynn Milner.

With special thanks to Julian McIntosh at Safariquip, The Stones, Castleton, Derbyshire (tel: 01433 620 320) for the loan of equipment for photography; and to Holmfirth Cycles, Holmfirth, Yorkshire for the loan of cycling equipment; and to Andrew Morrison for the loan of additional camping items.

PICTURE CREDITS

All photography in this book is the copyright of Anness Publishing Ltd except for the following:
t = top; c = centre; b = bottom;
l = left; r = right
**Corbis** p91t, p94t; **Simon Dodd** p11b, p18t, p75tl, p75tm, p75tr, p79b; **Peter G. Drake** p1, p6tr, p7 (both),10b, p13b, p14b, p16, p18b, p19 (both), p21 (both), p22, p23 (both), p27b, p32, p33 (both), p35b, p36, p37tl, p42t, p49t, p52t, p52br, p53br, p60t, p67tl, p67tr, p70 (both), p71tl, p73 (both), p78b, p86t, p88, p89 (all), p90 (all), p92t, p93 (both), p94b, p95b.